HISTORICAL MANNEQUIN COSTUMES

&

MYSTERIOUS MASKS

COLORING BOOK

Historical Mannequin COSTUMES Coloring Book

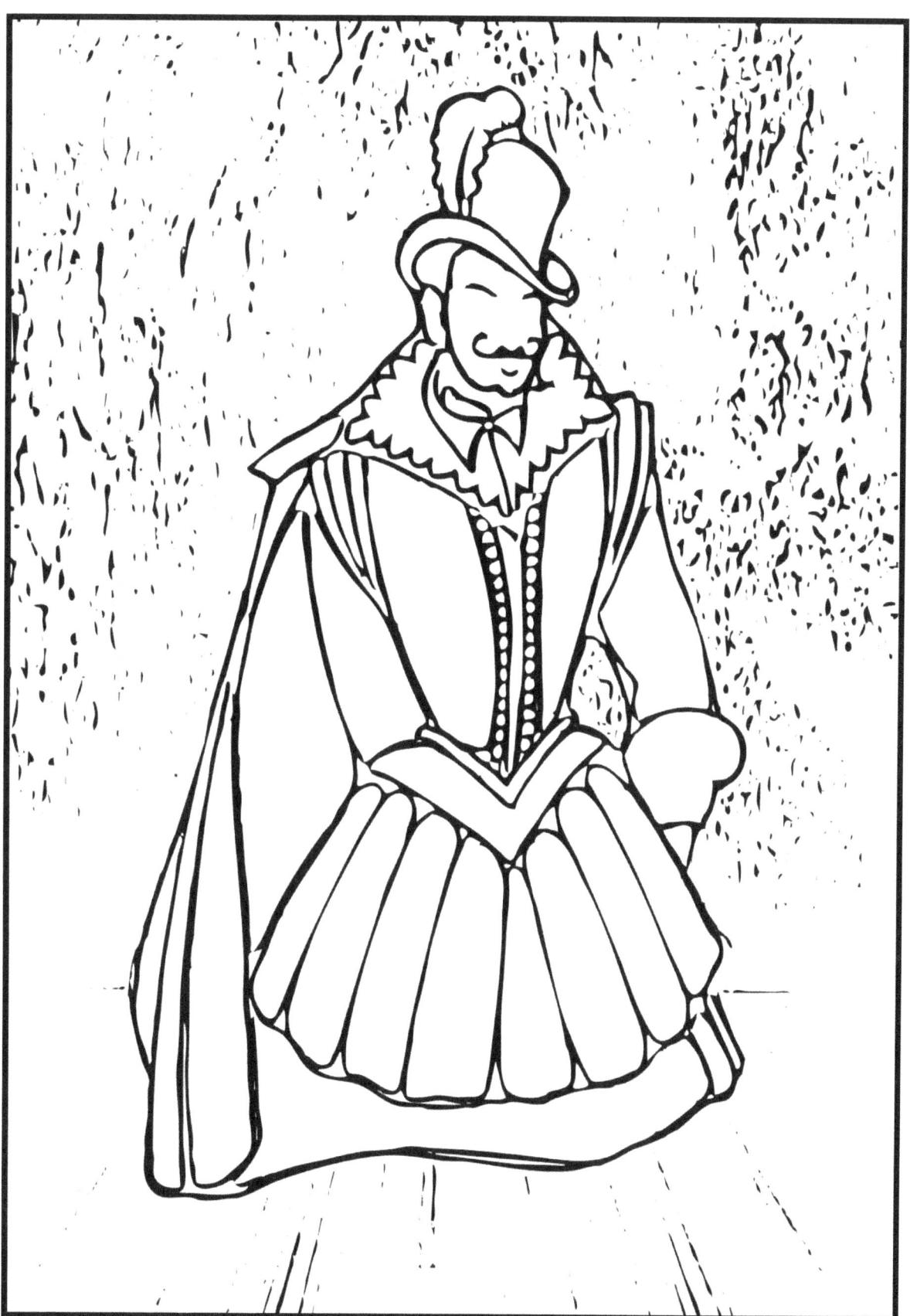

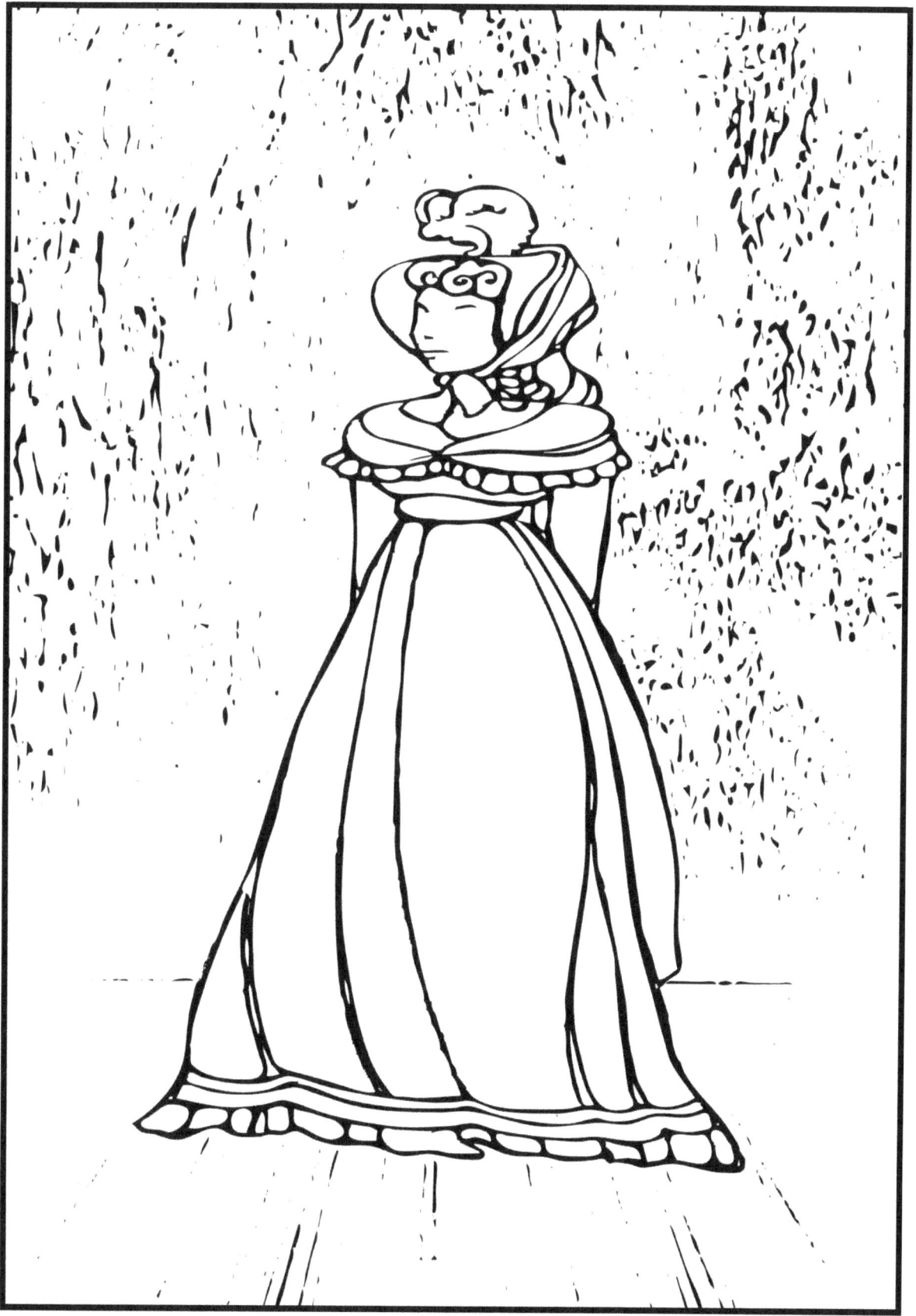

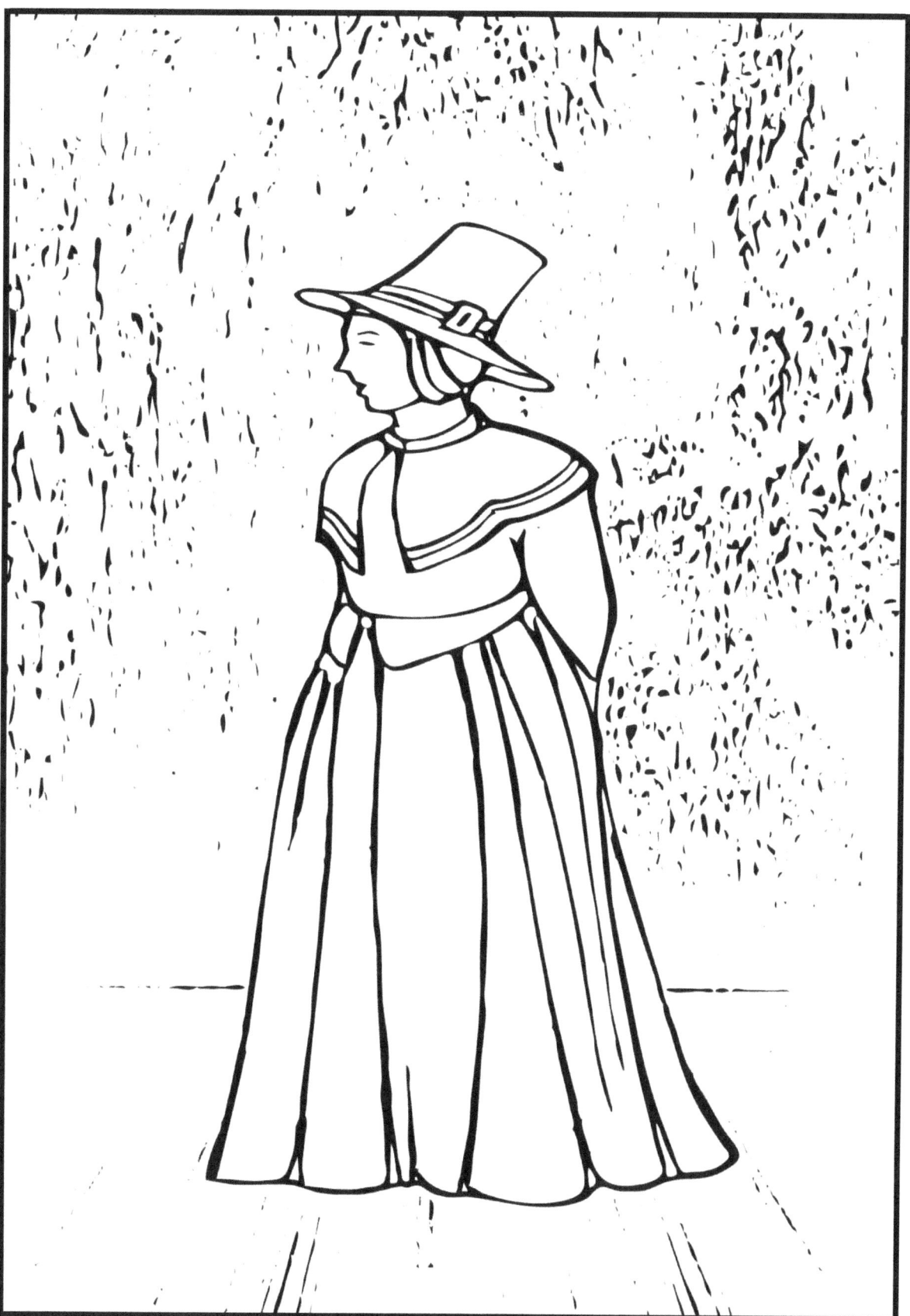

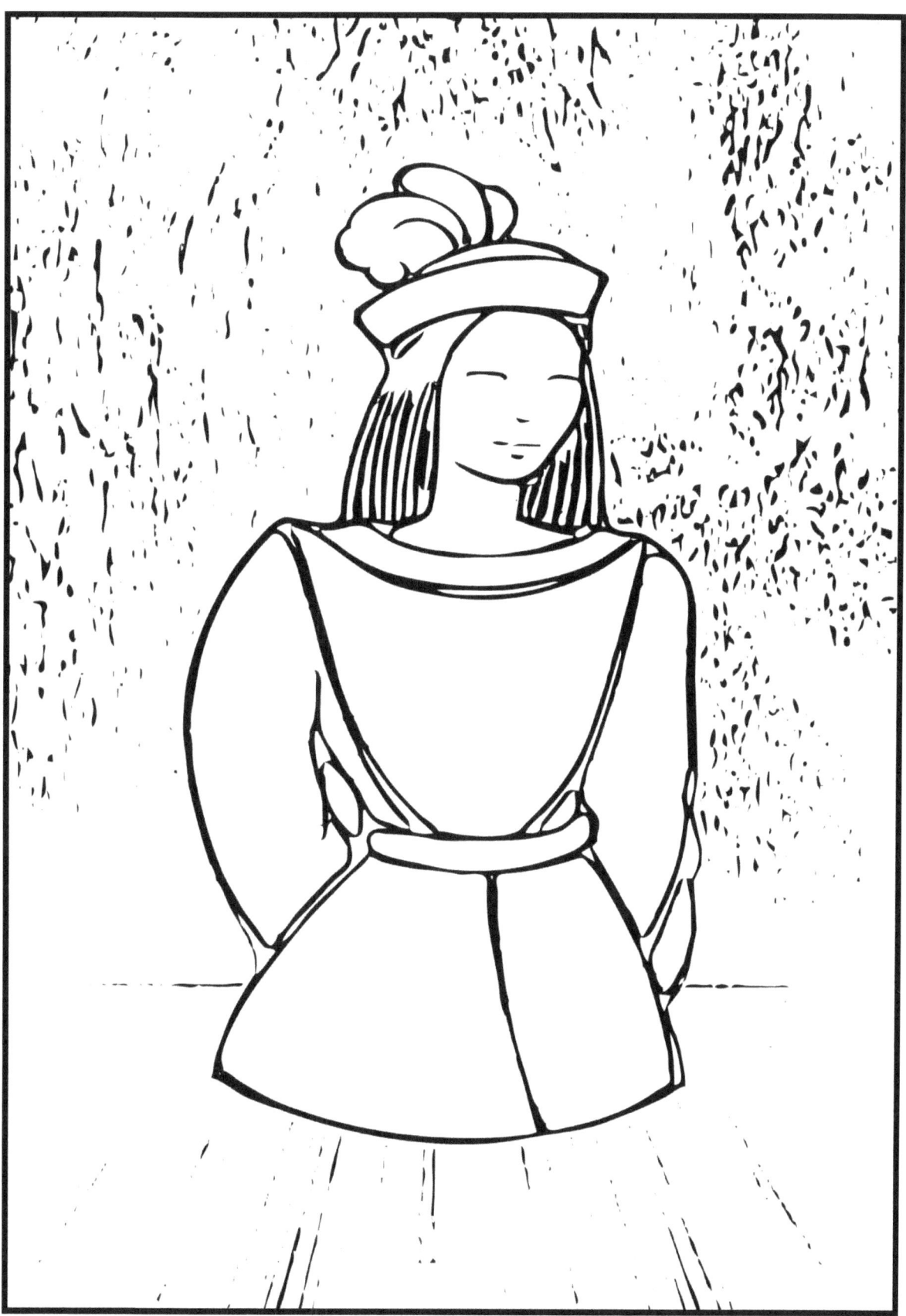

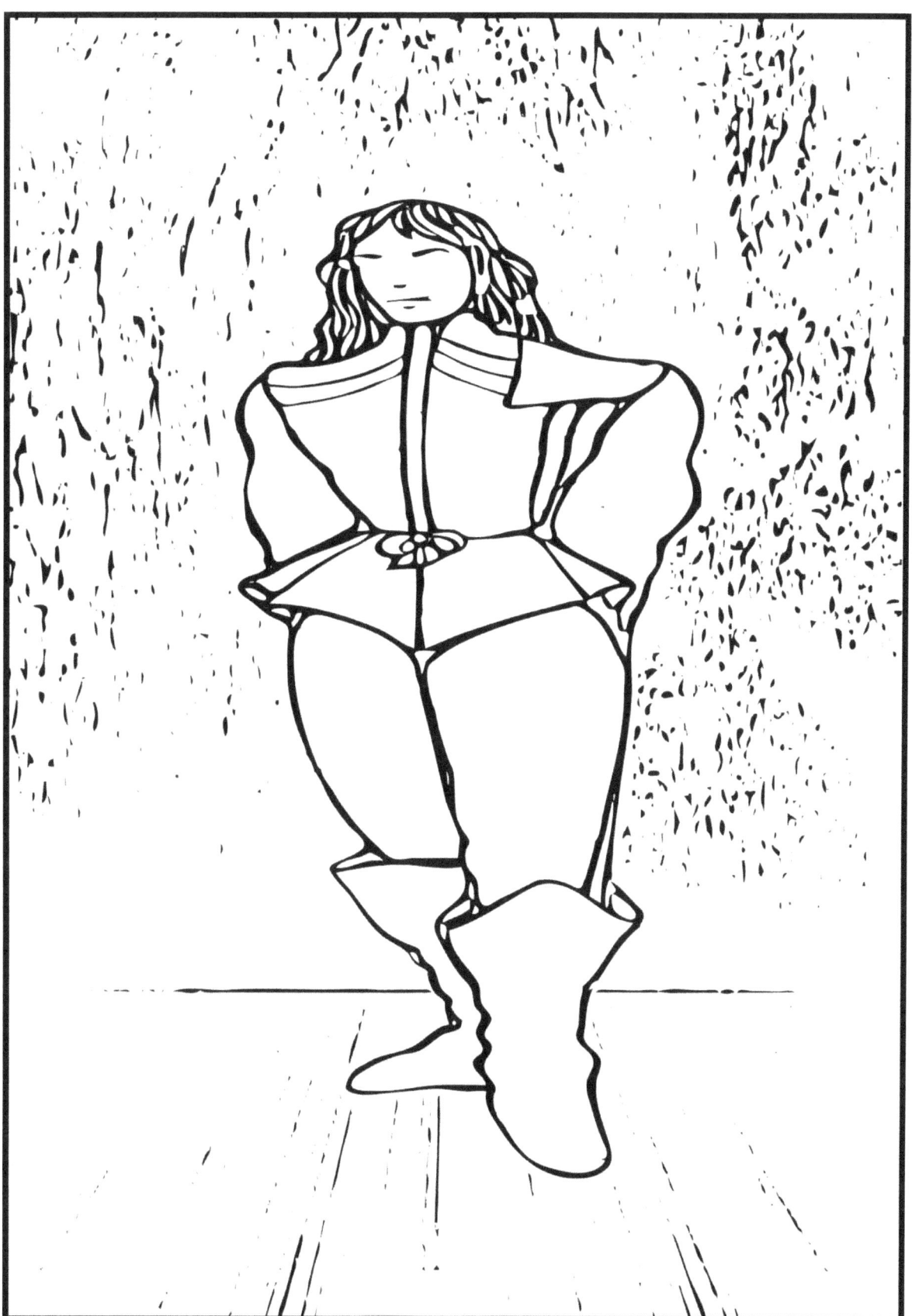

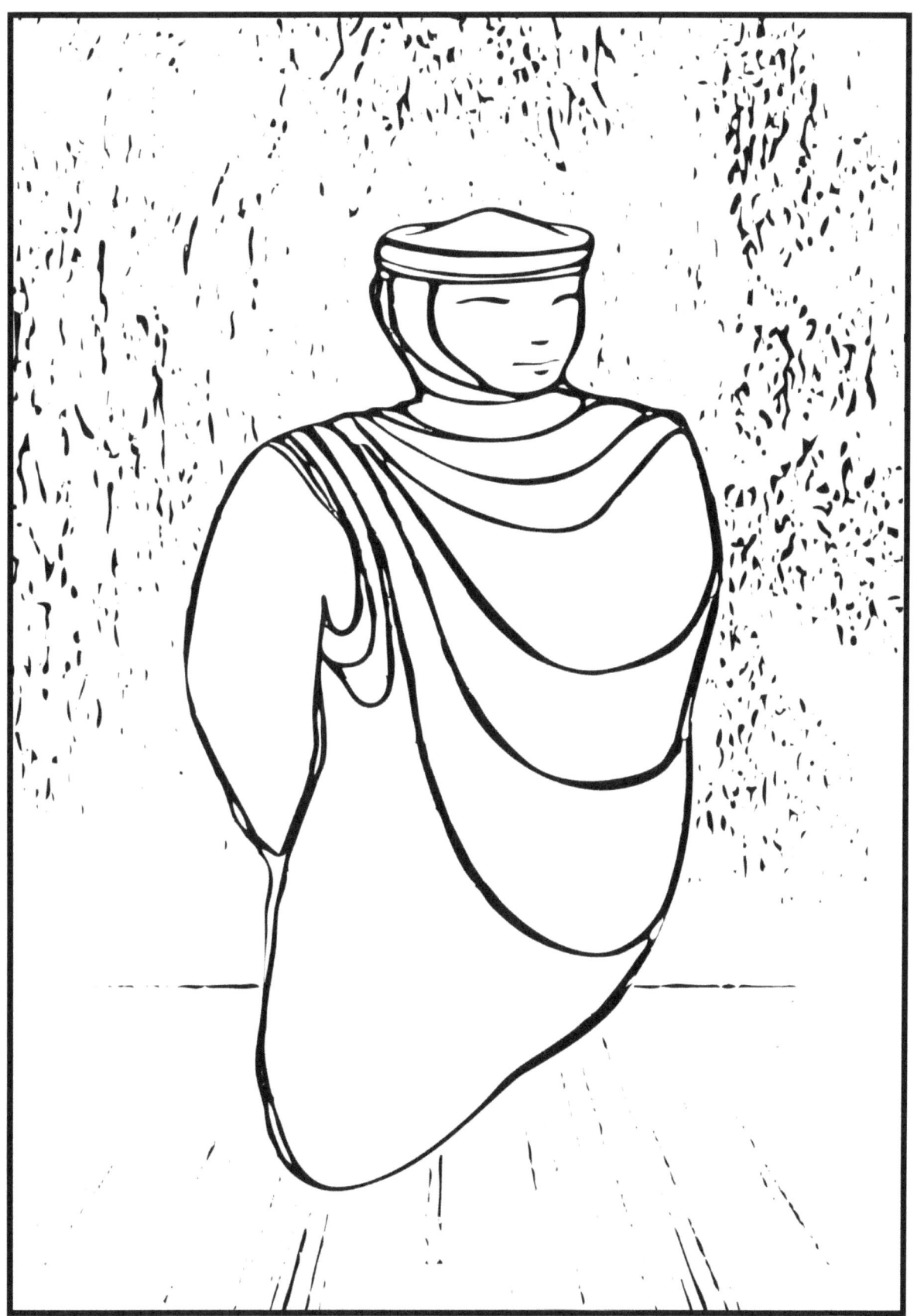

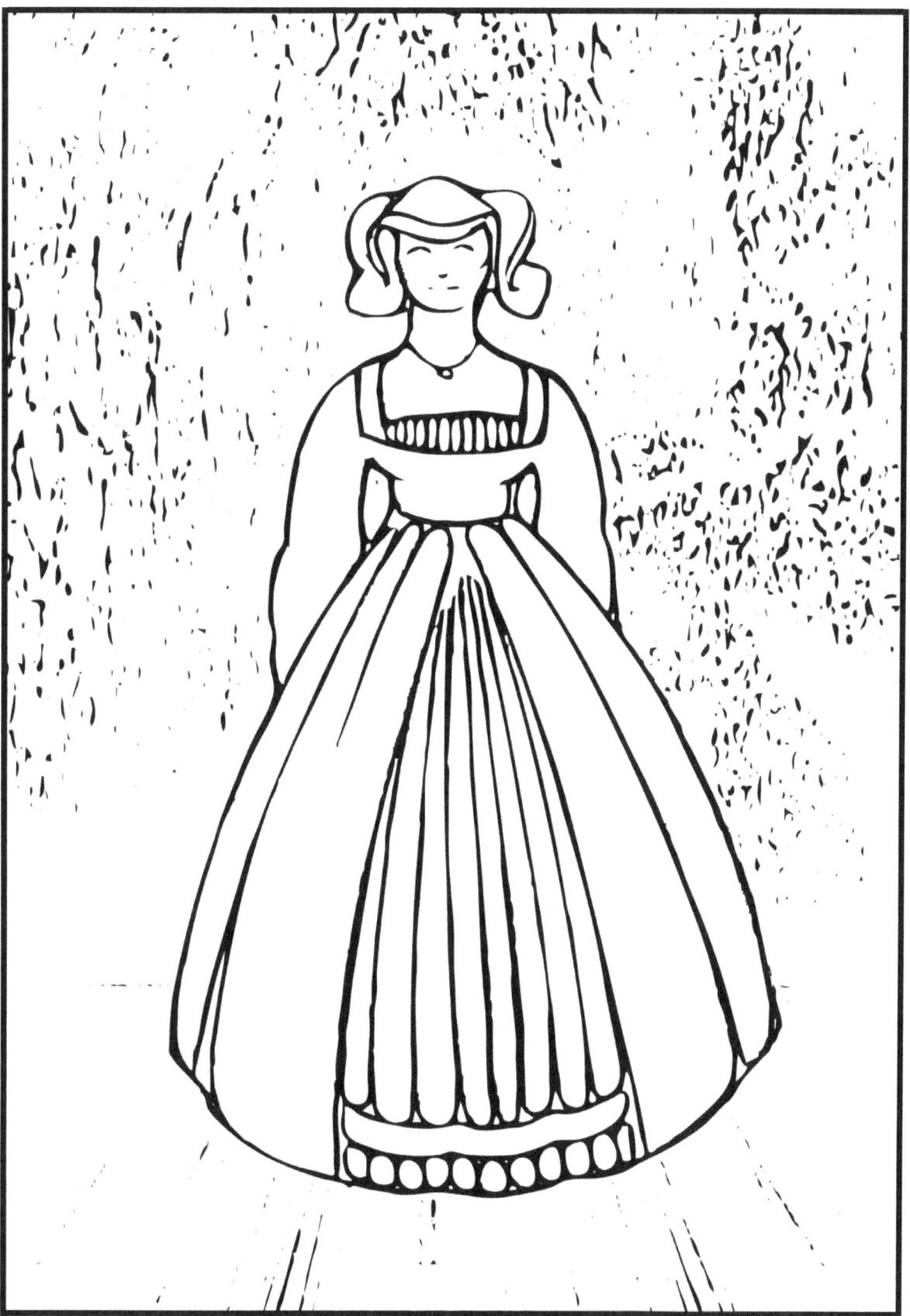

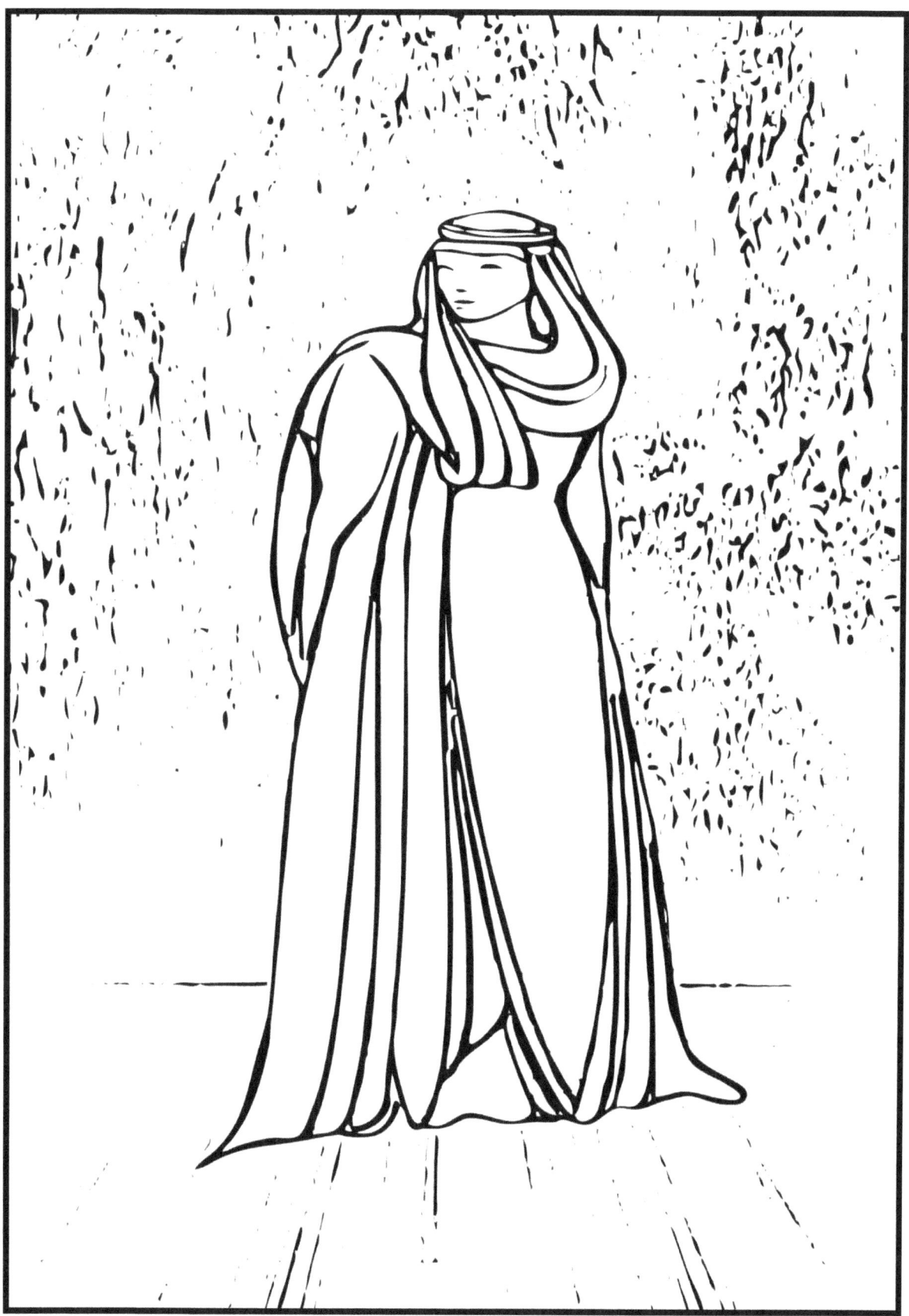

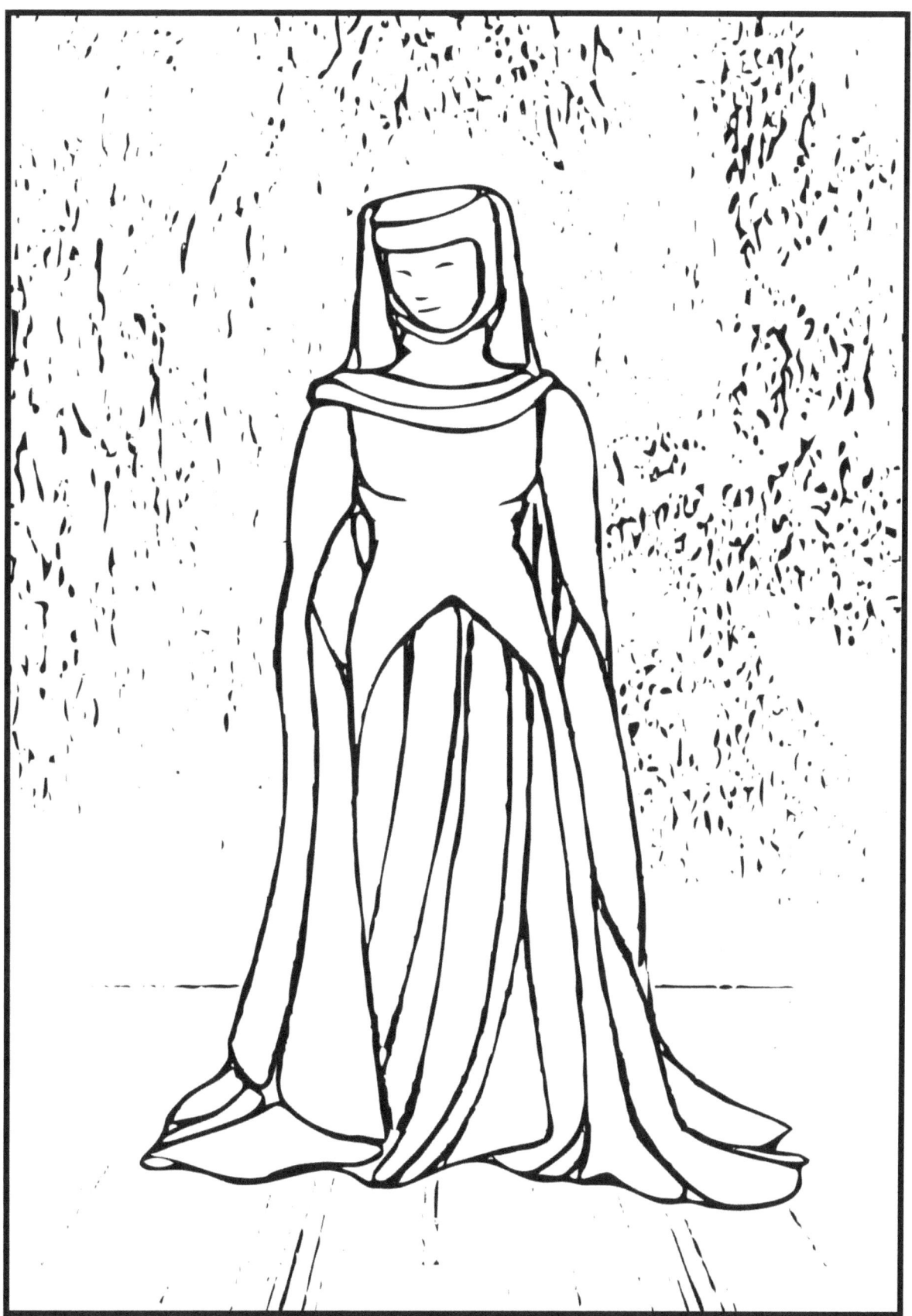

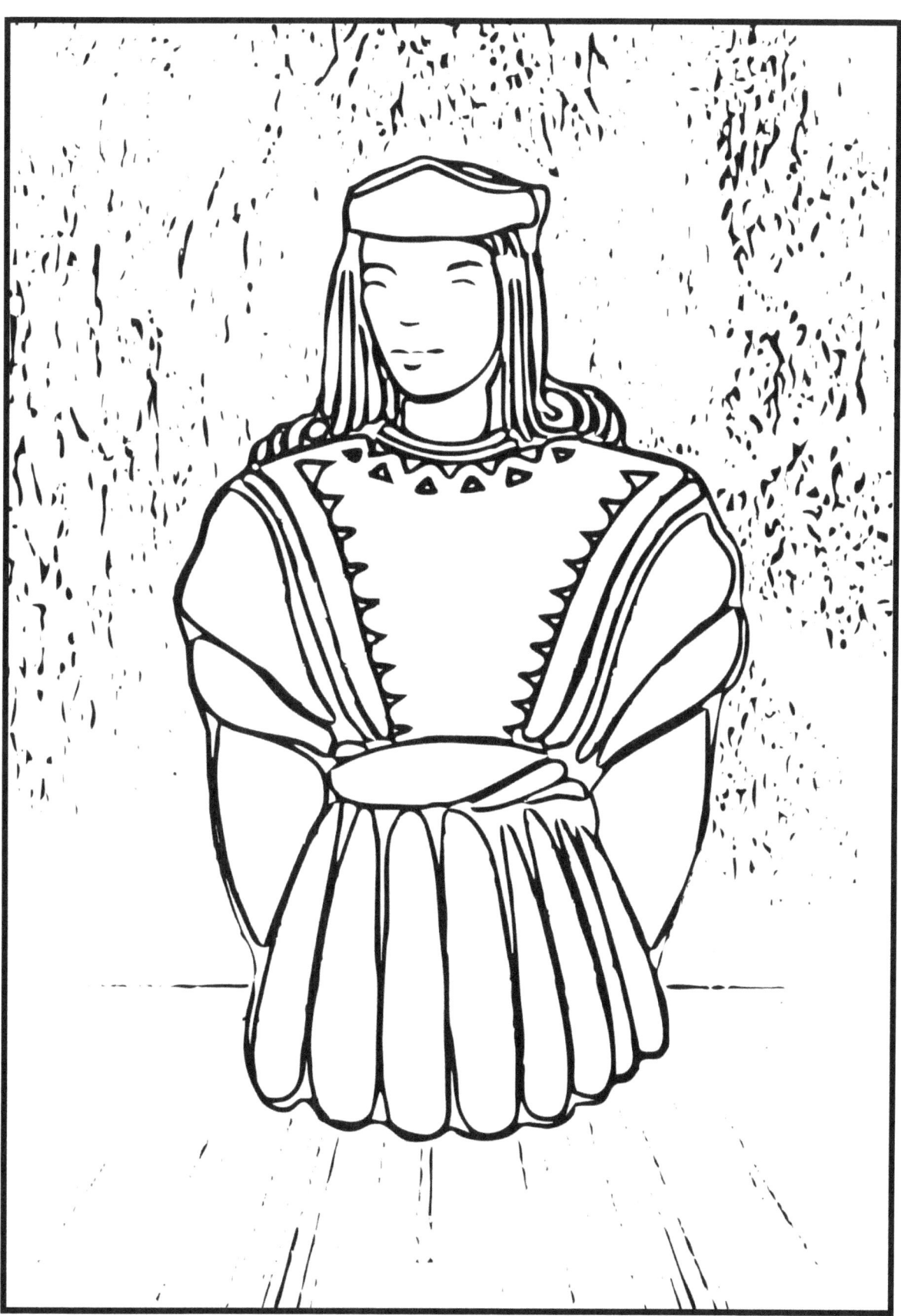

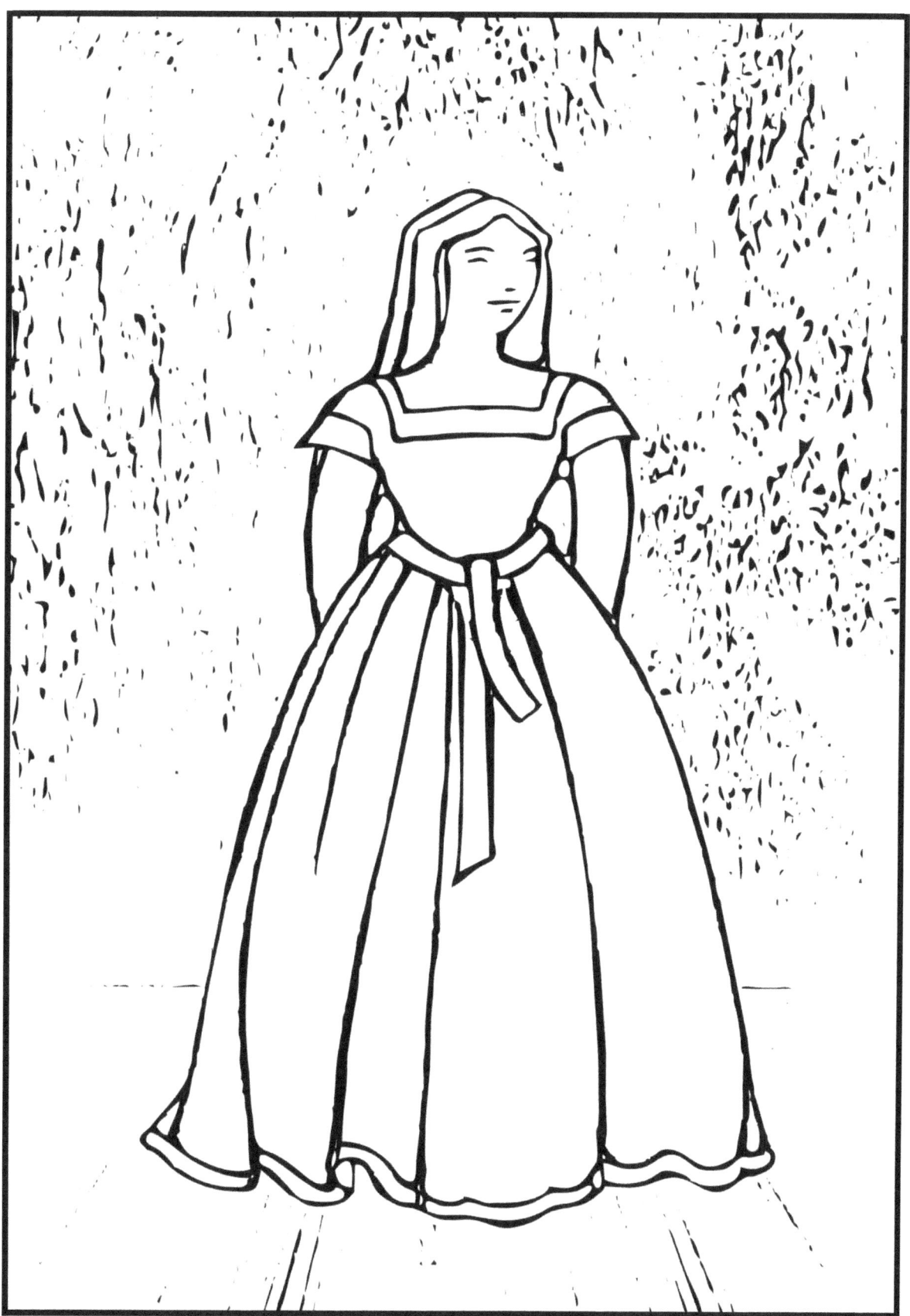

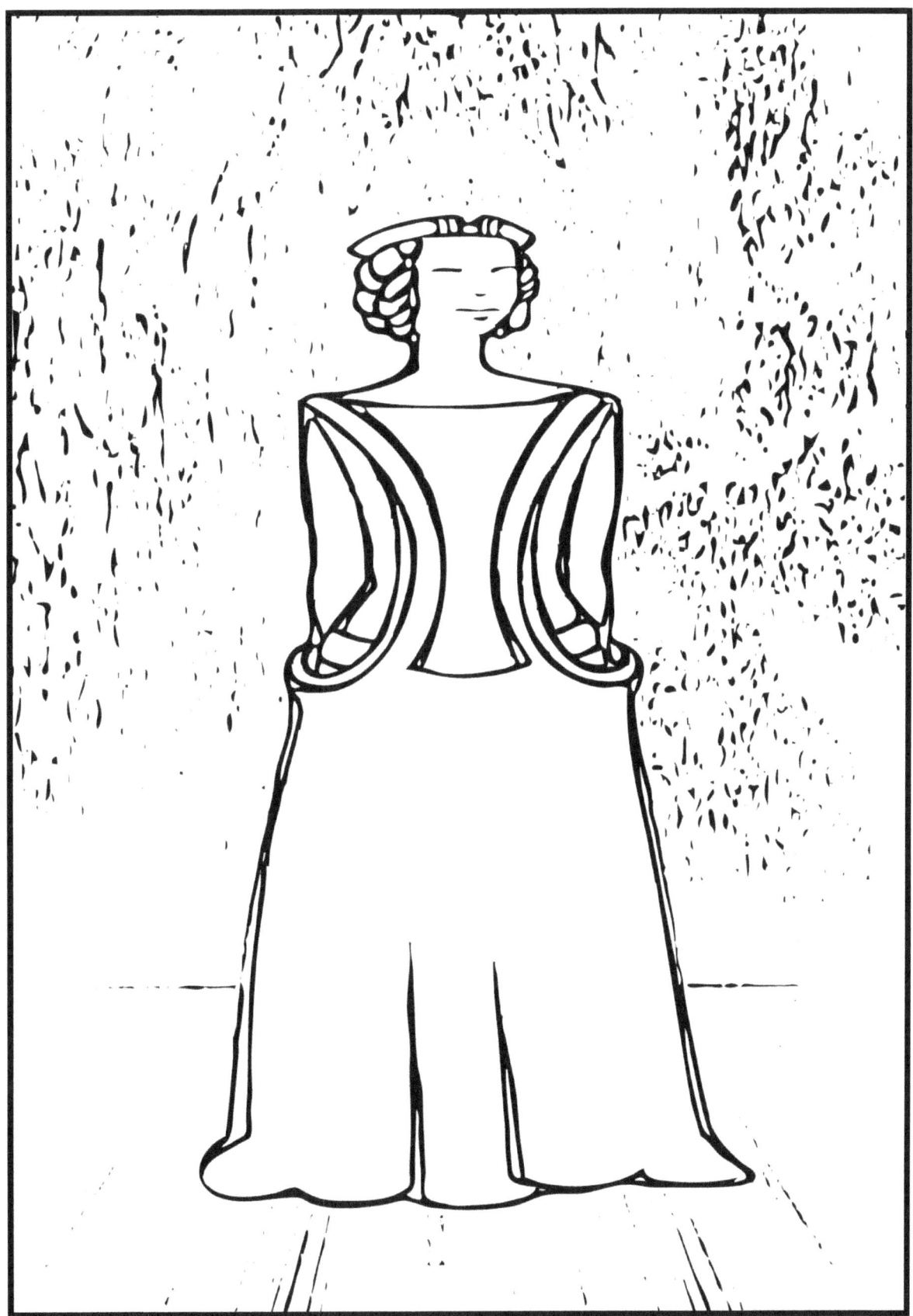

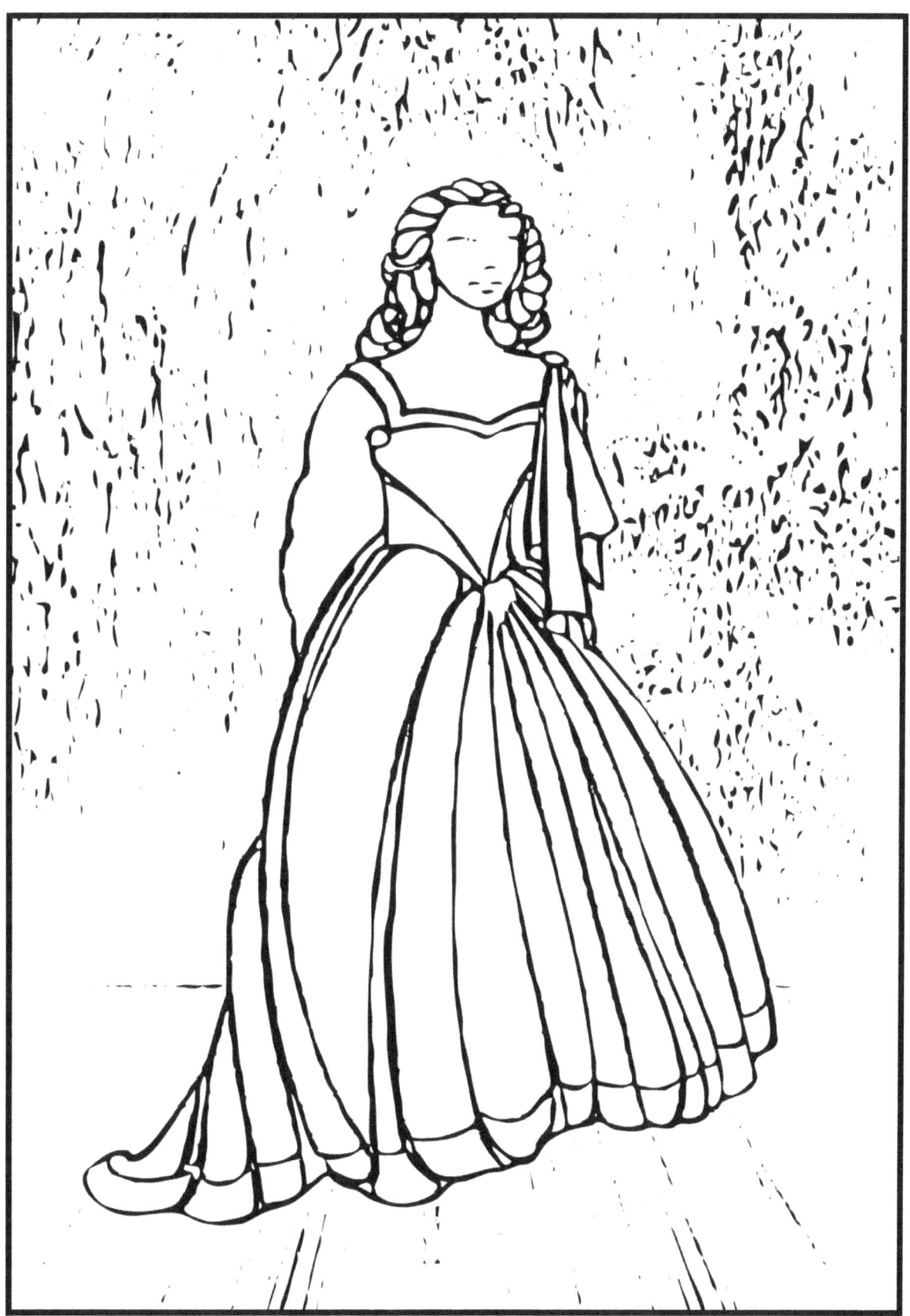

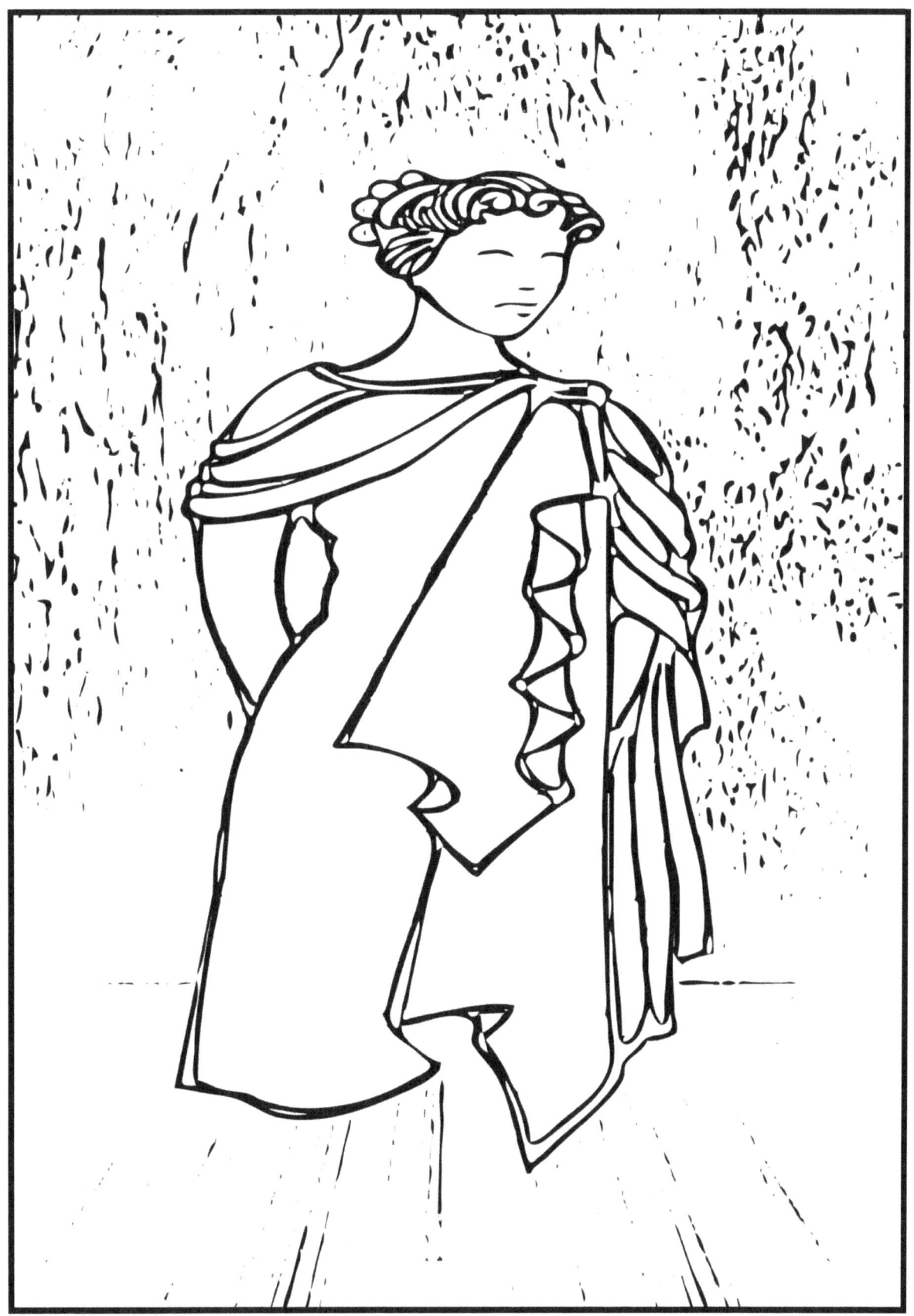

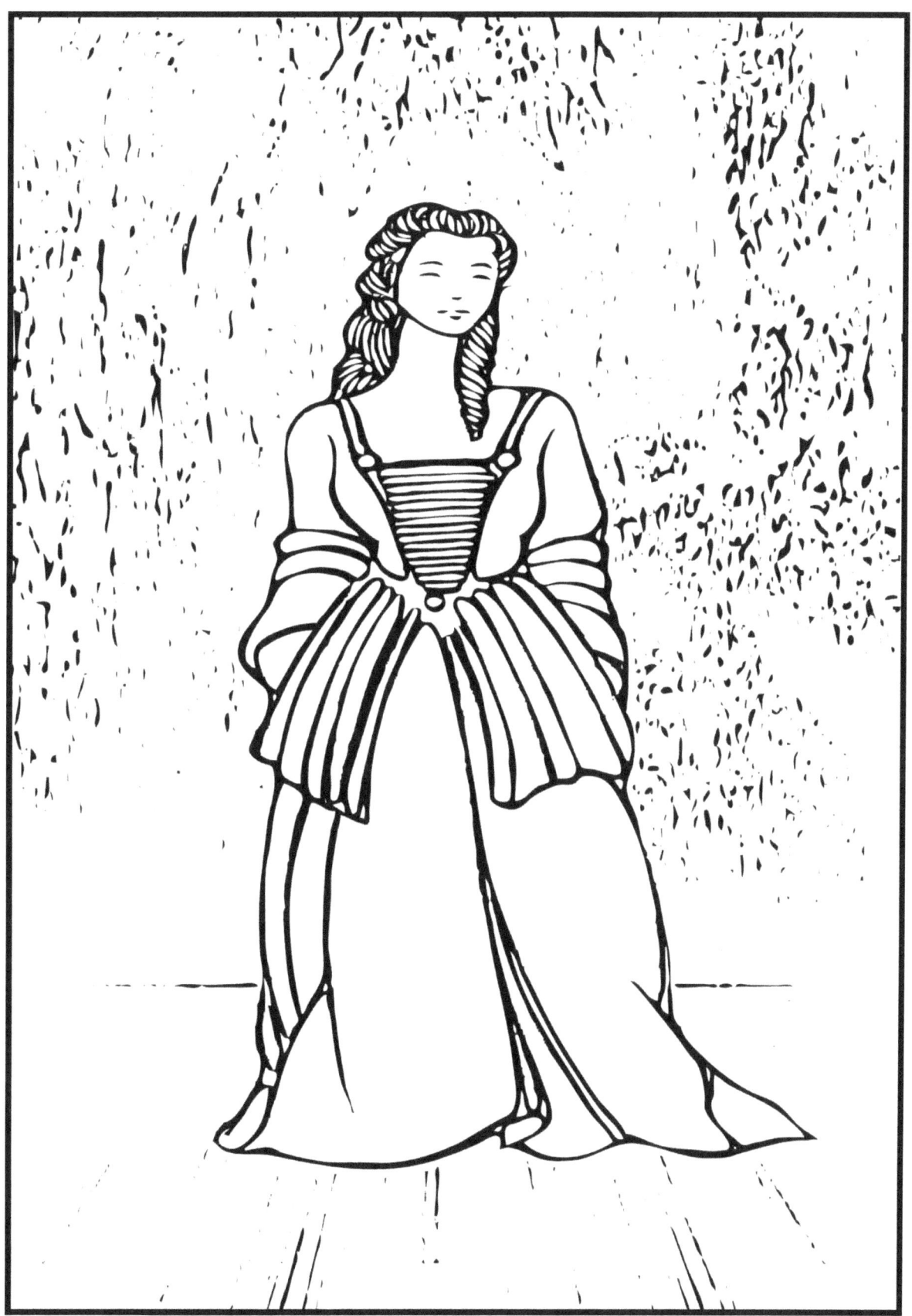

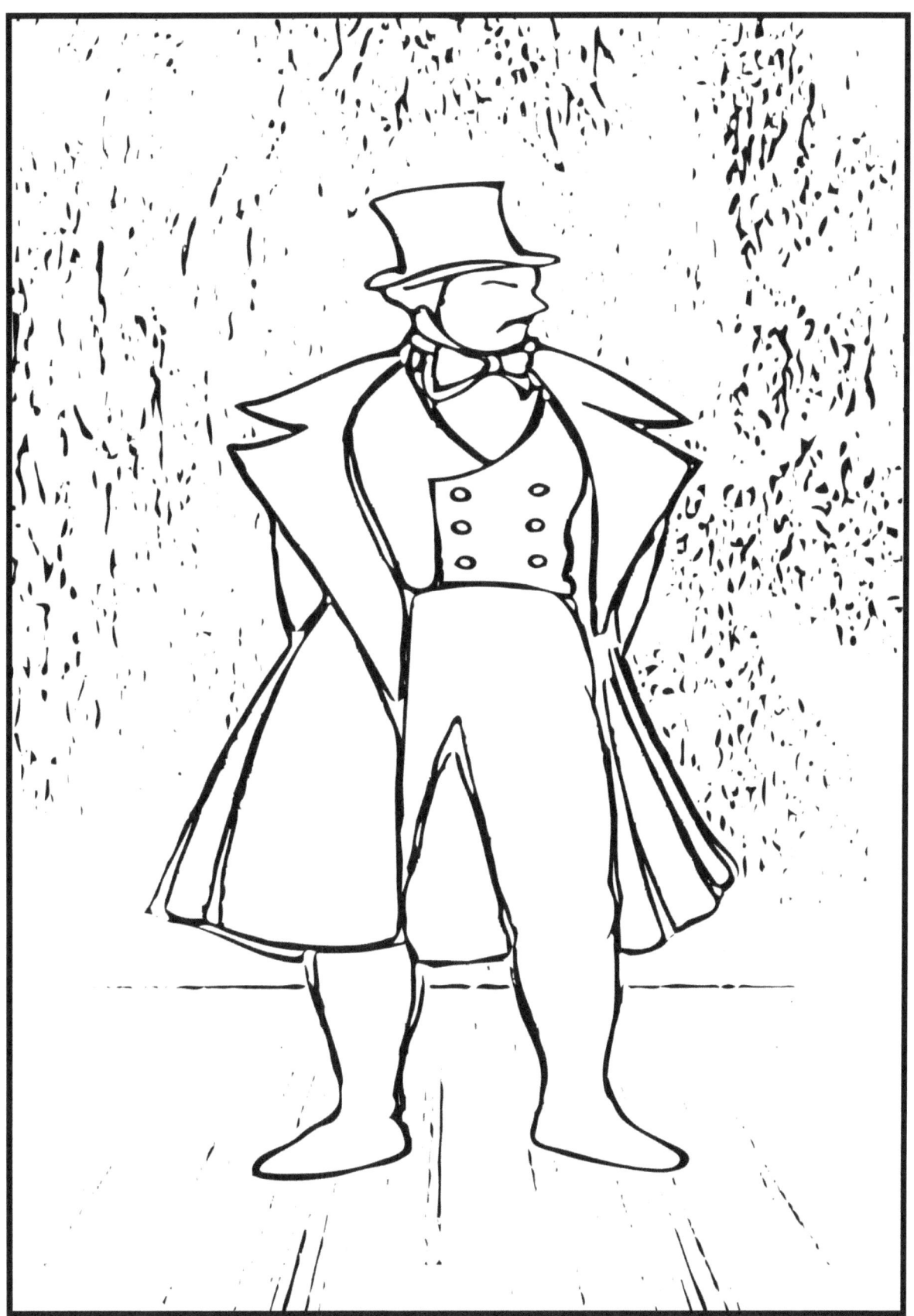

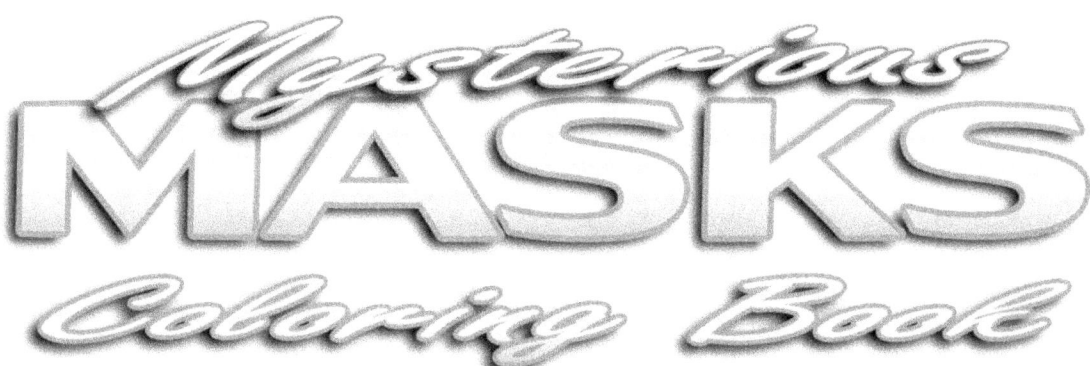

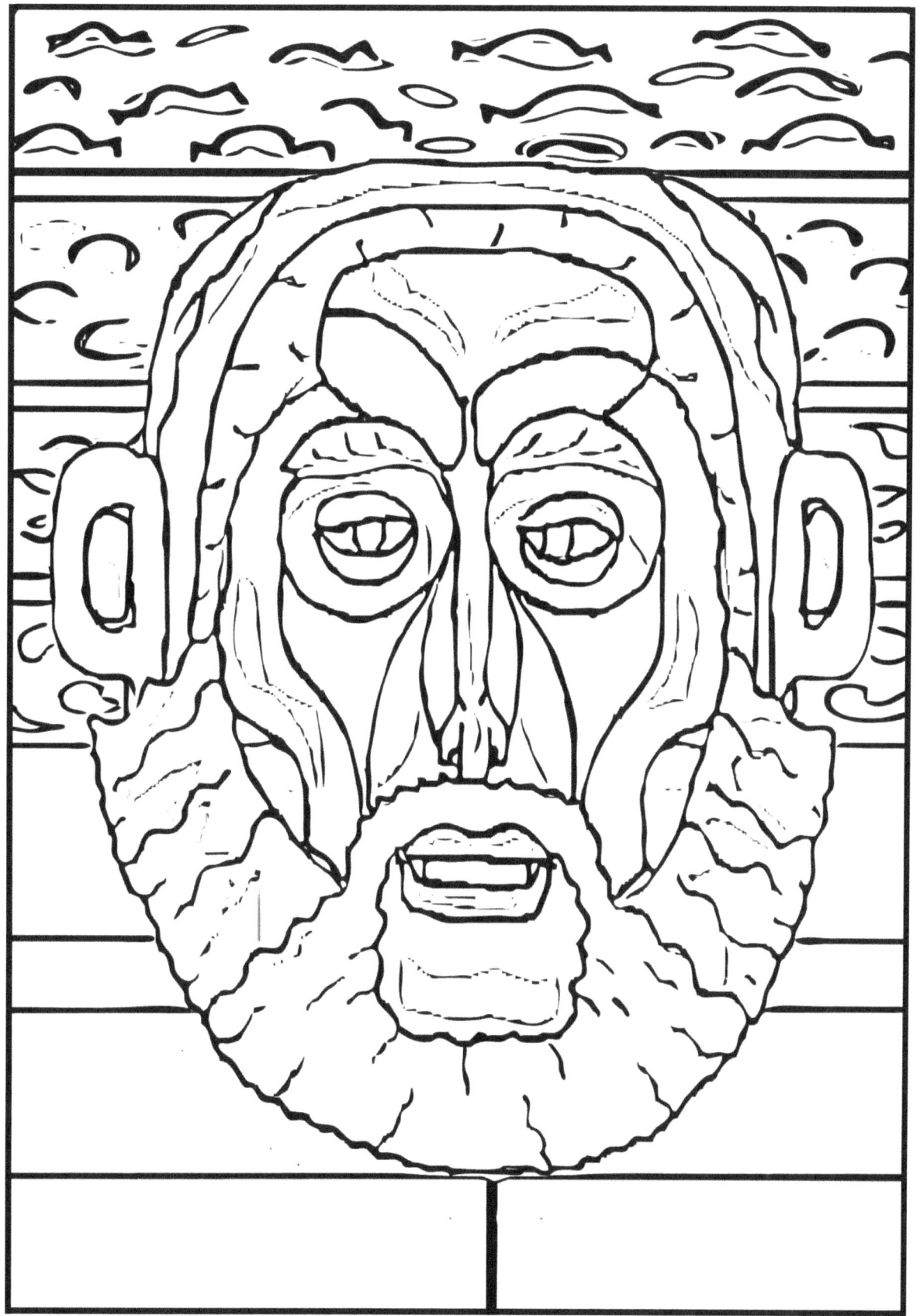

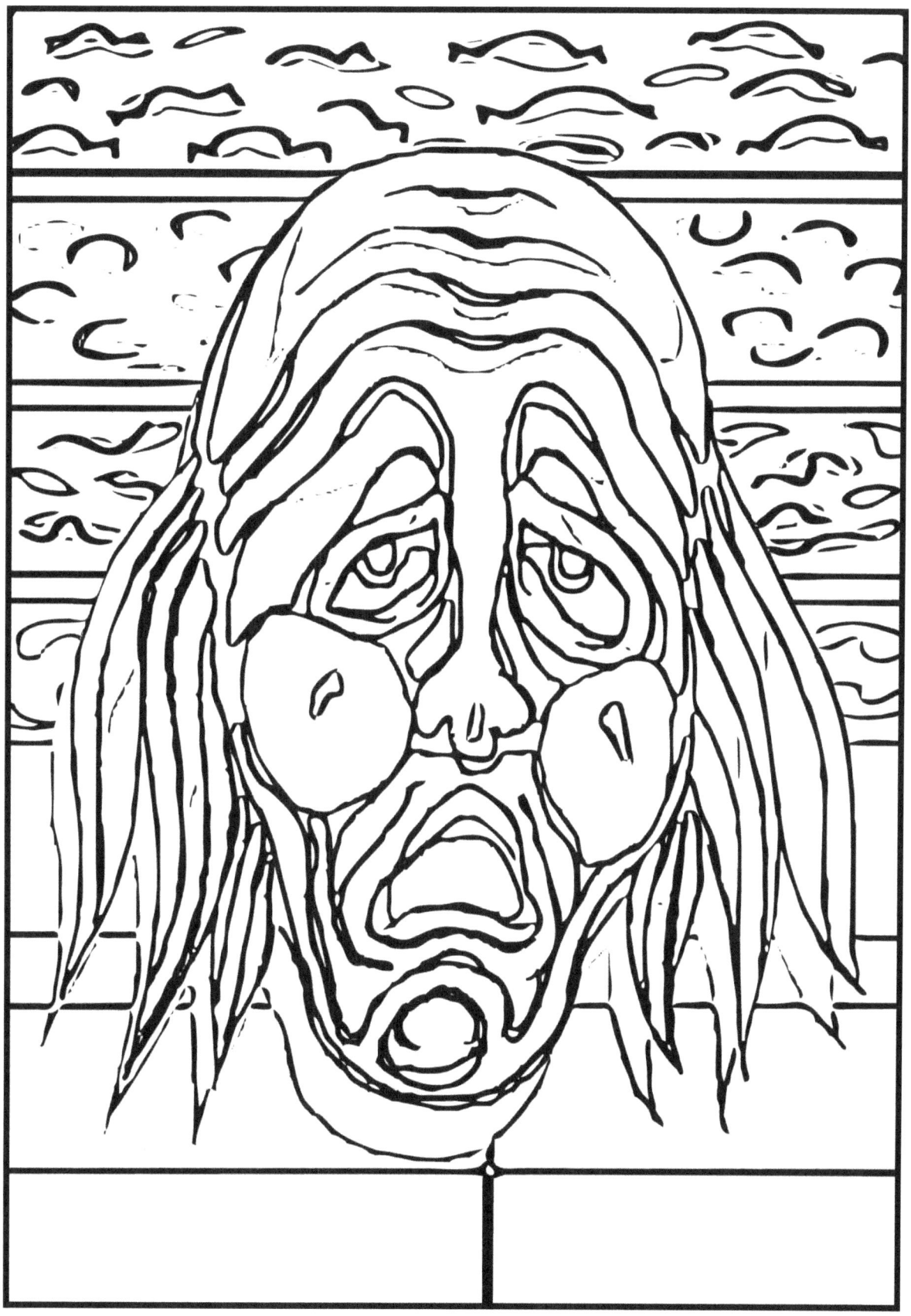

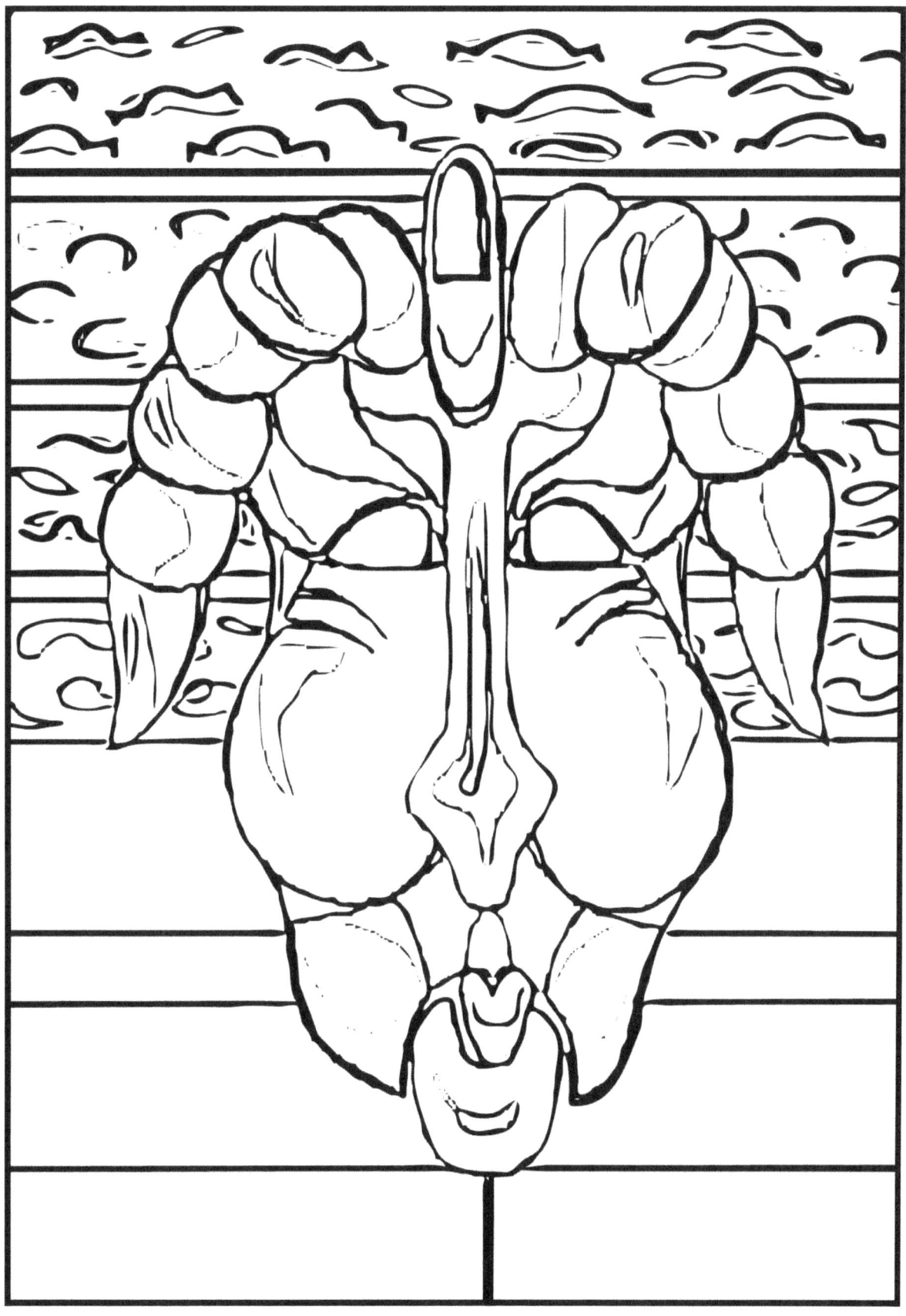

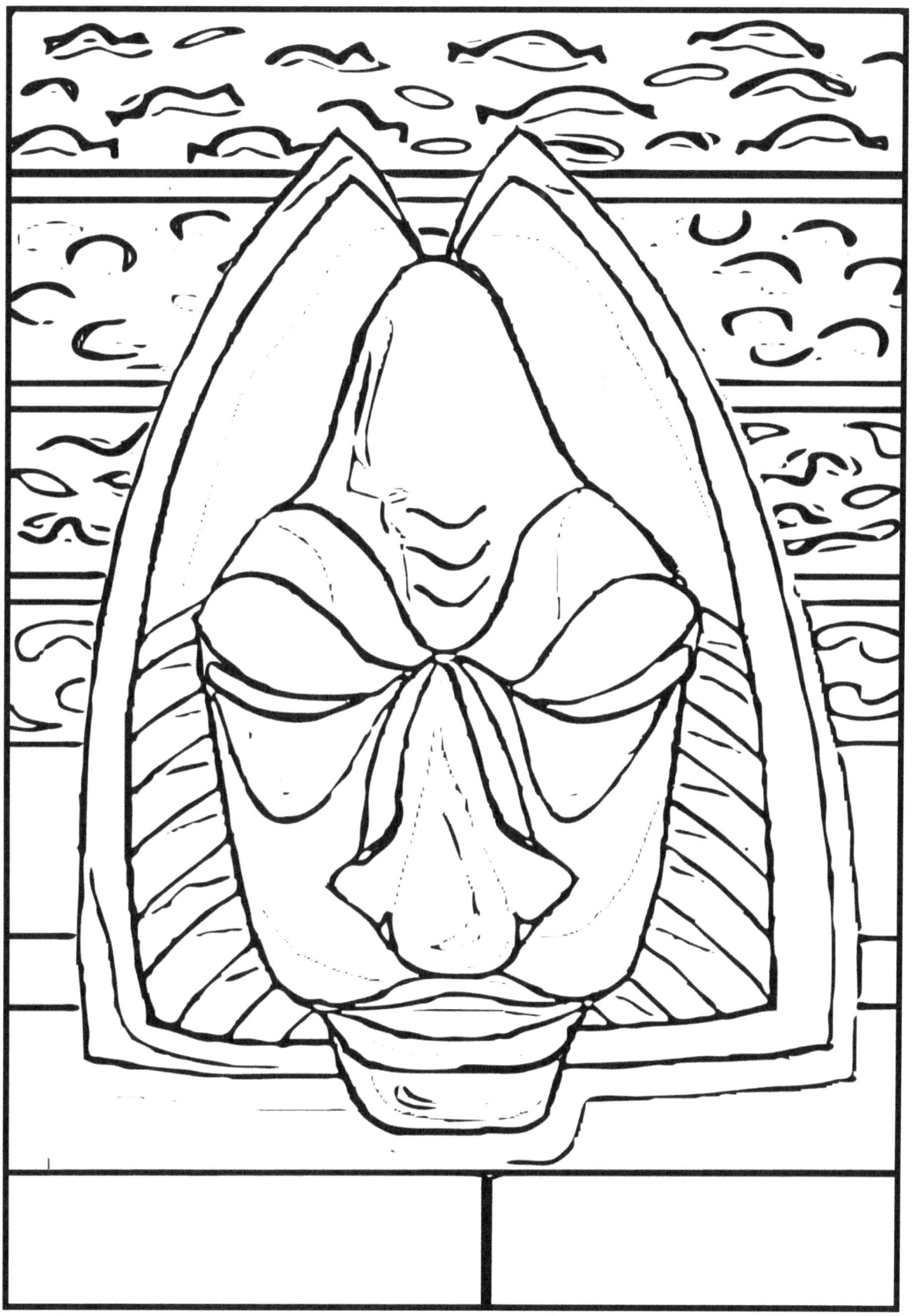

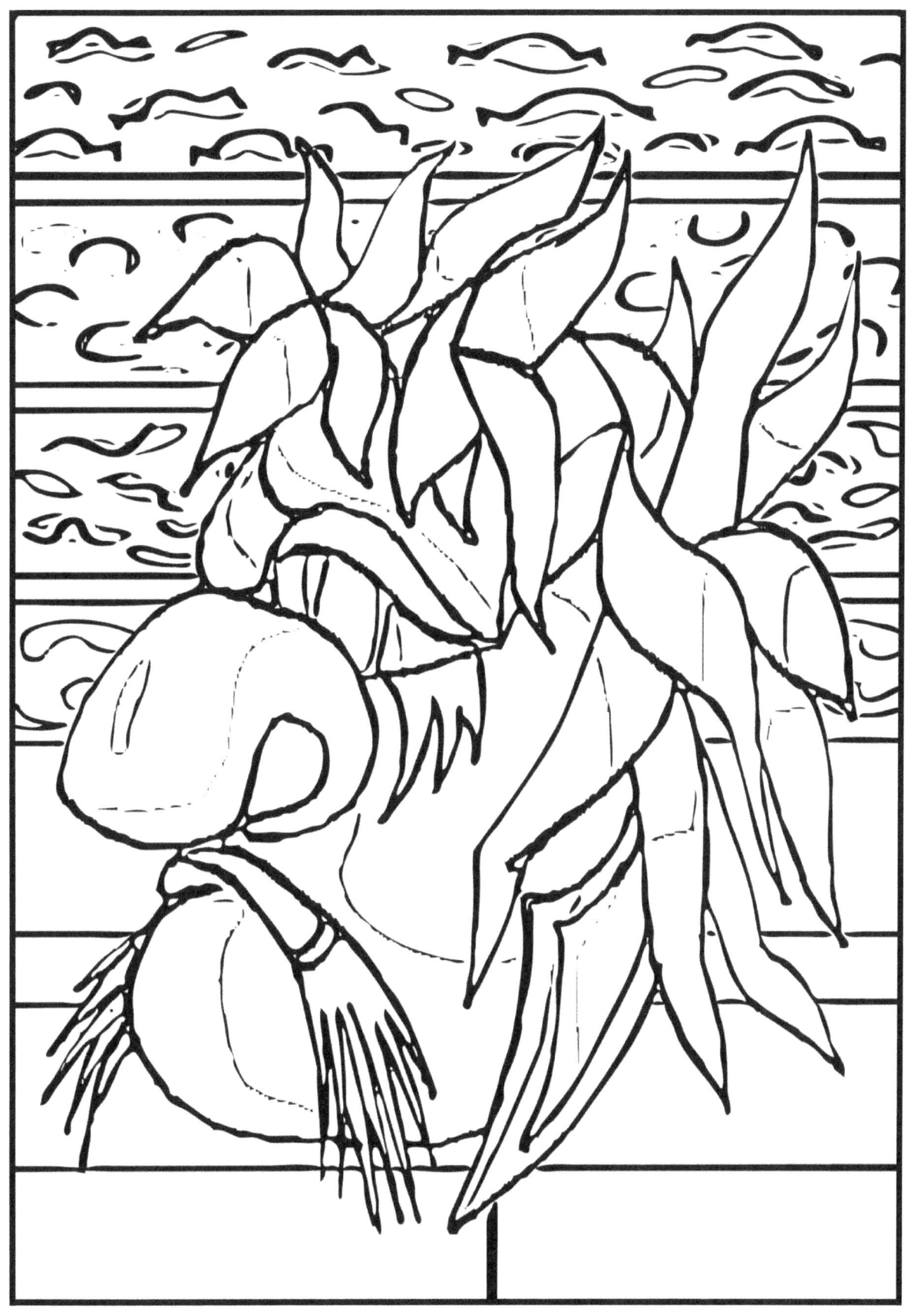

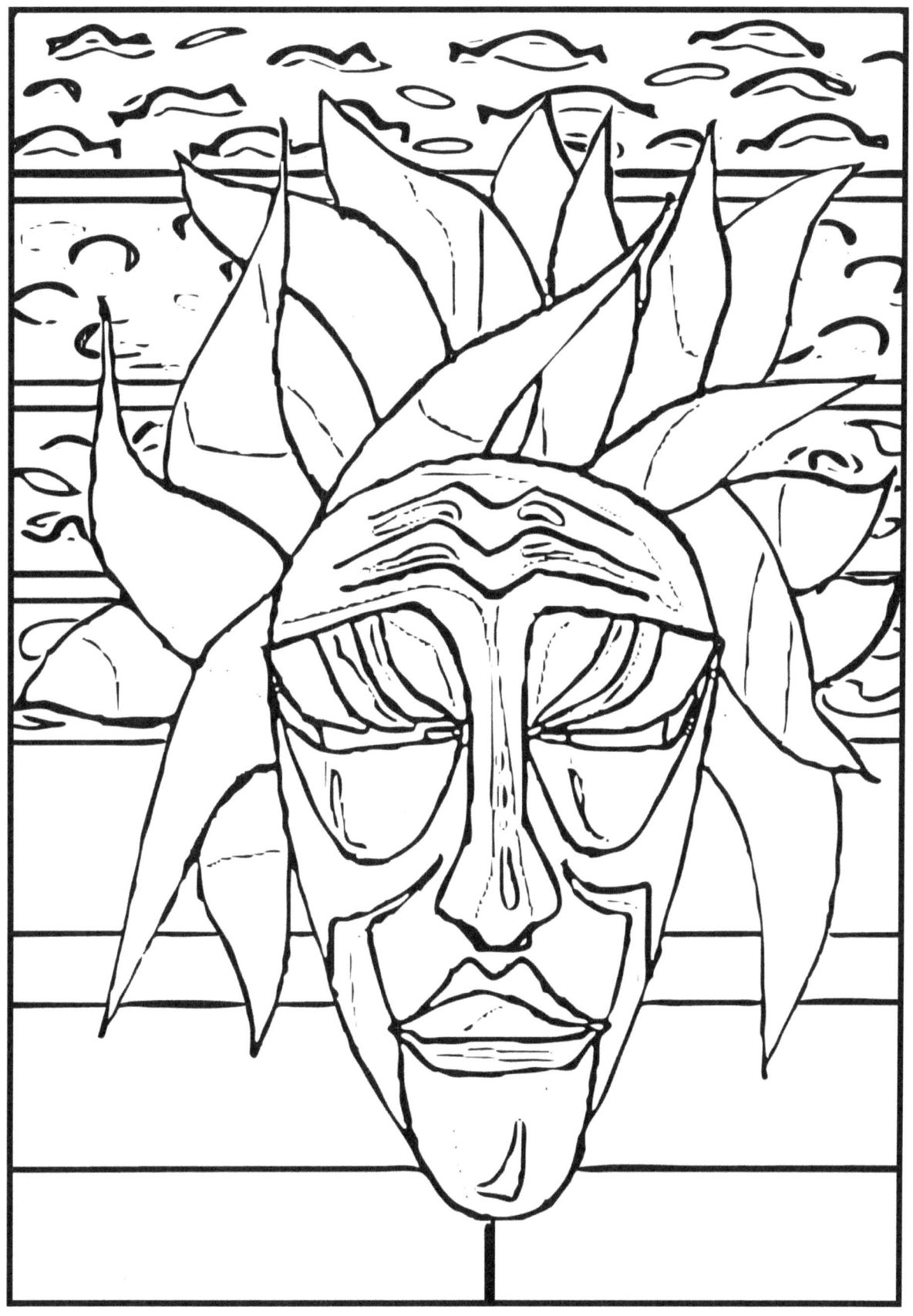

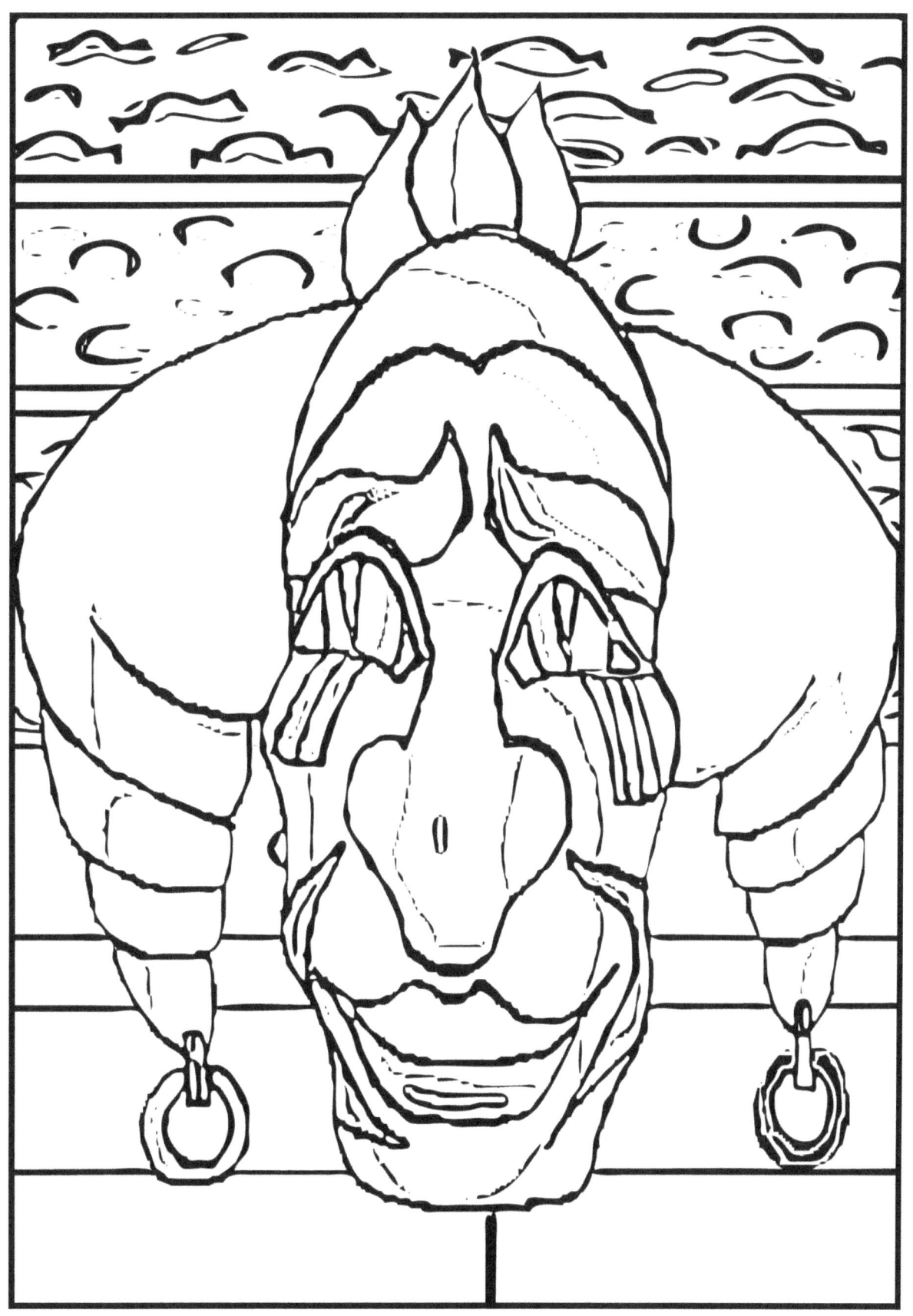

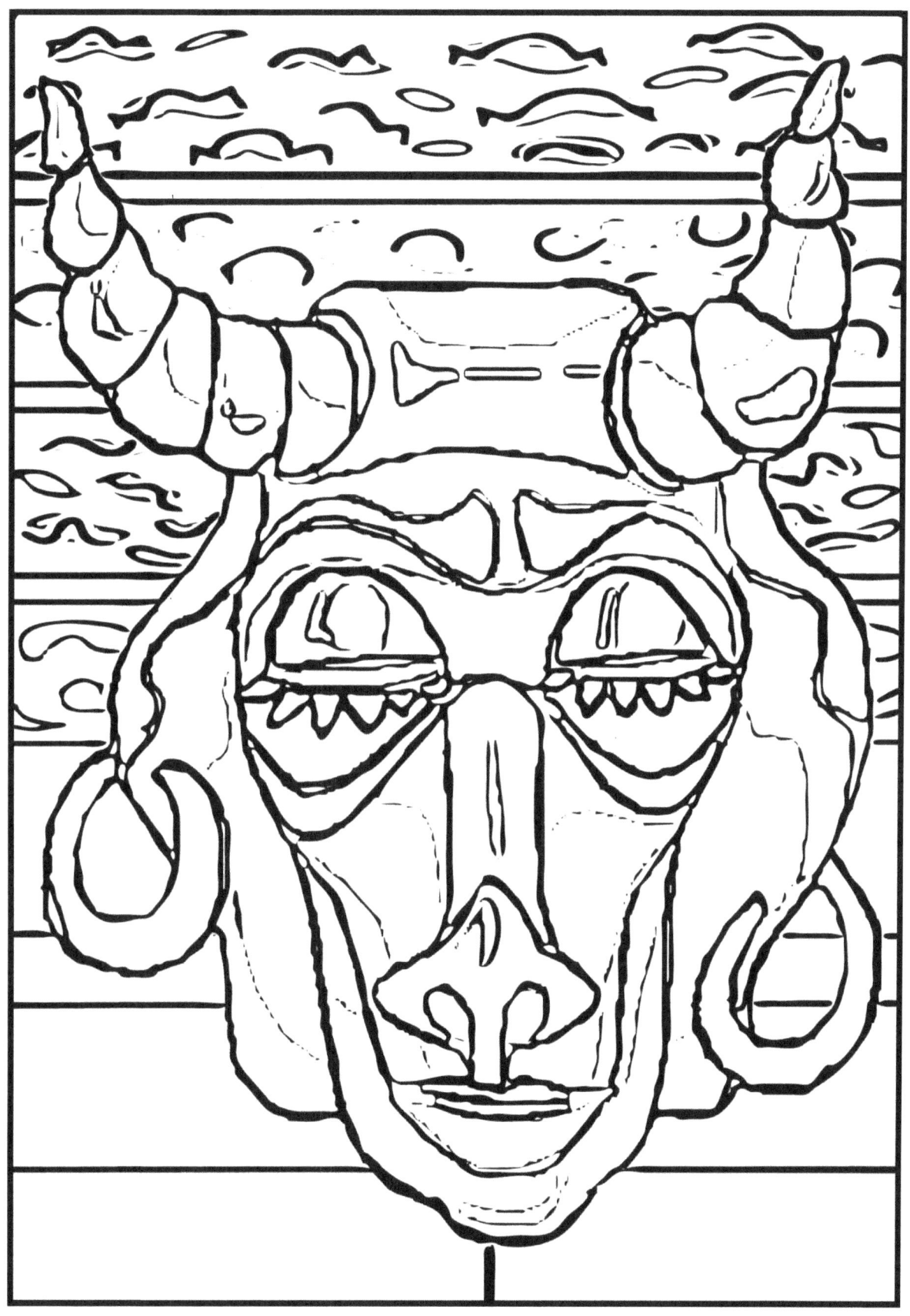

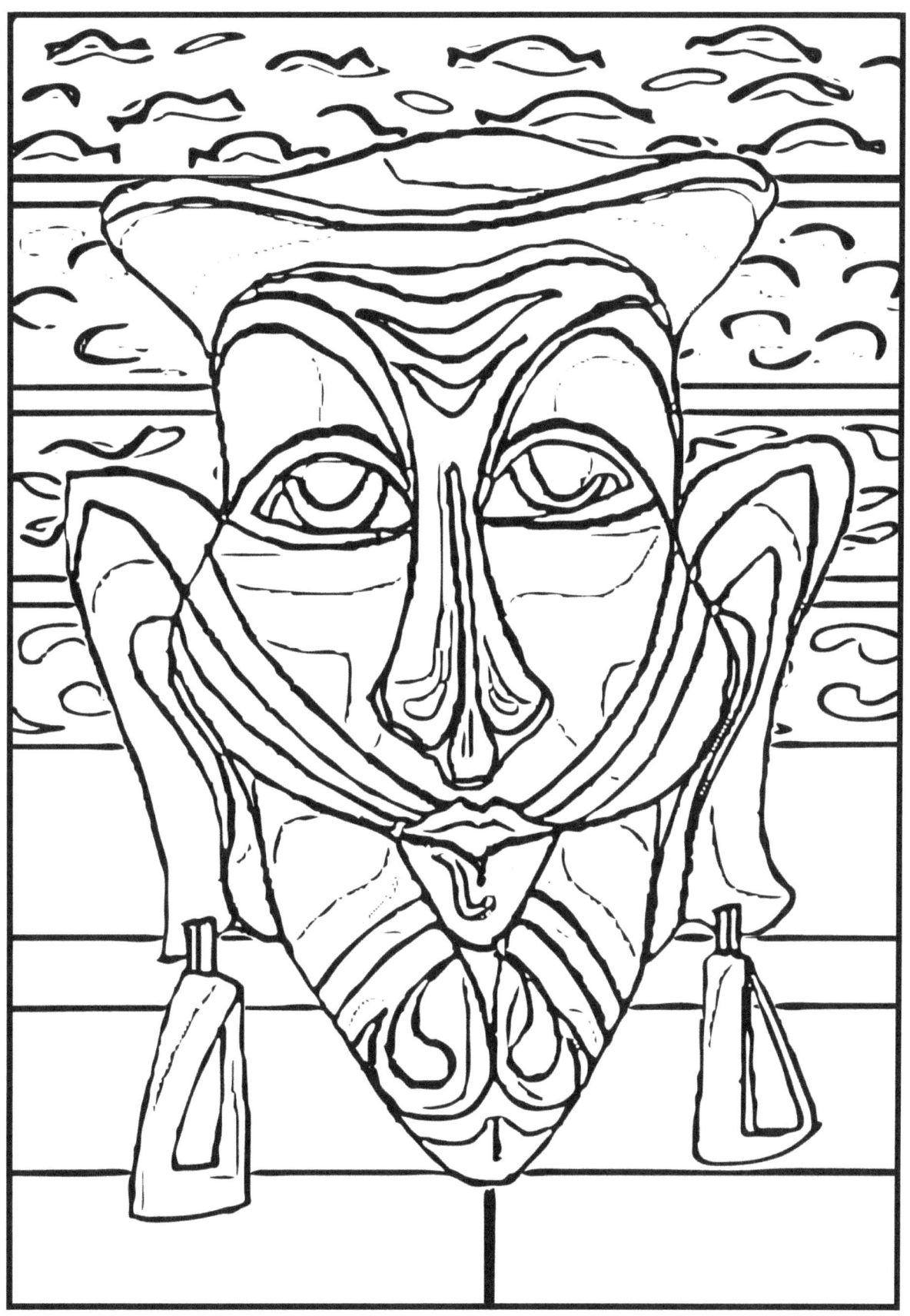

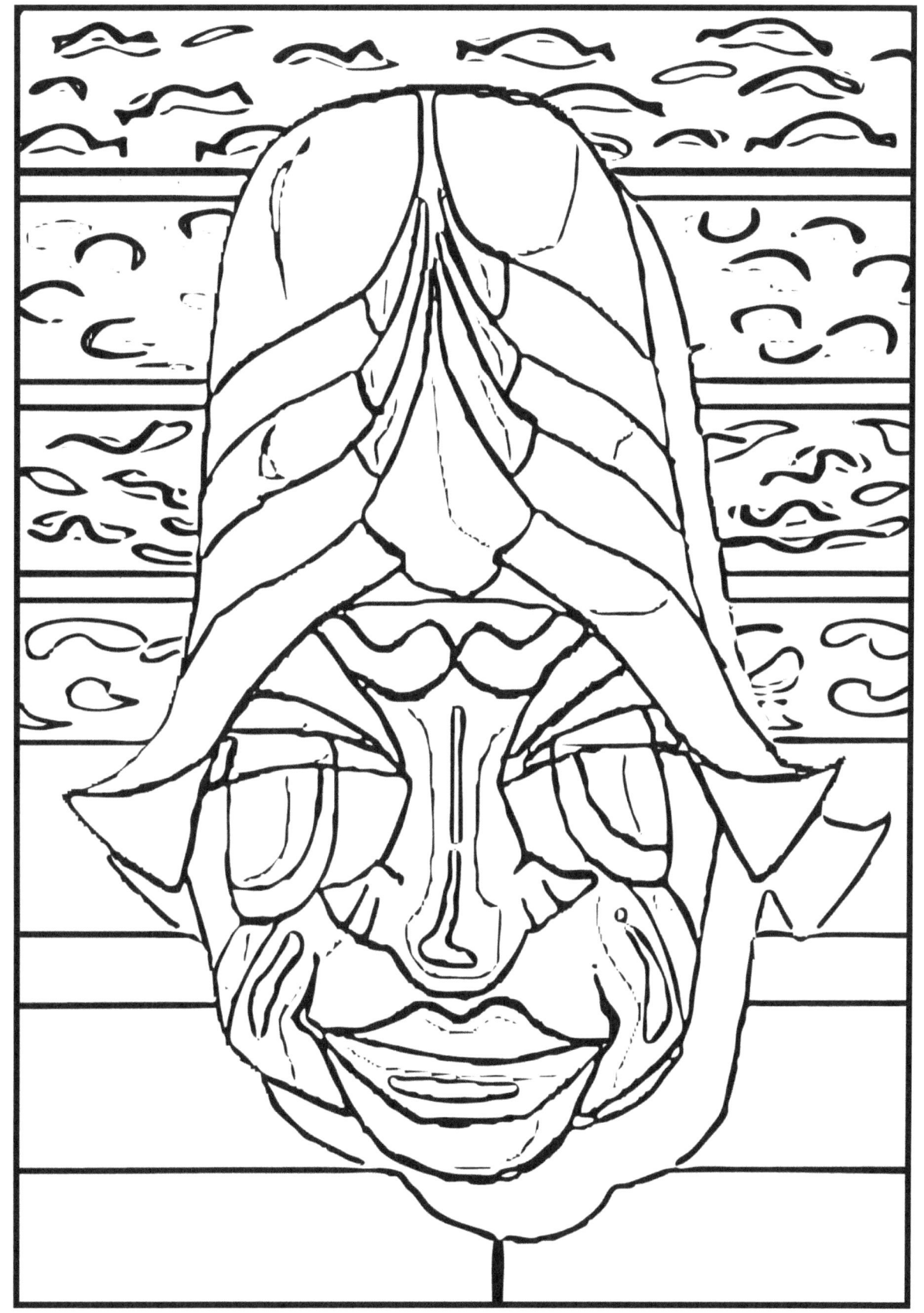

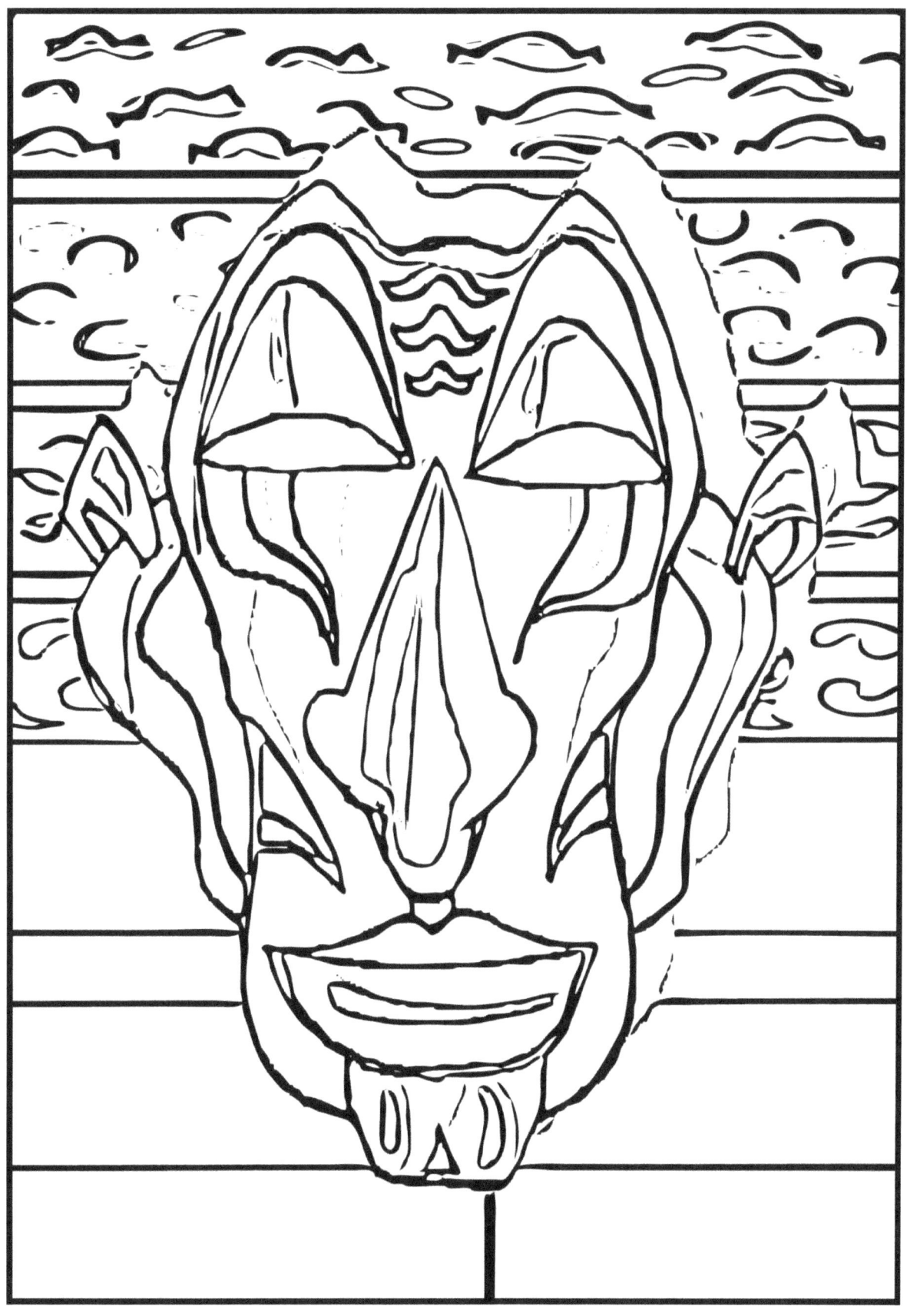

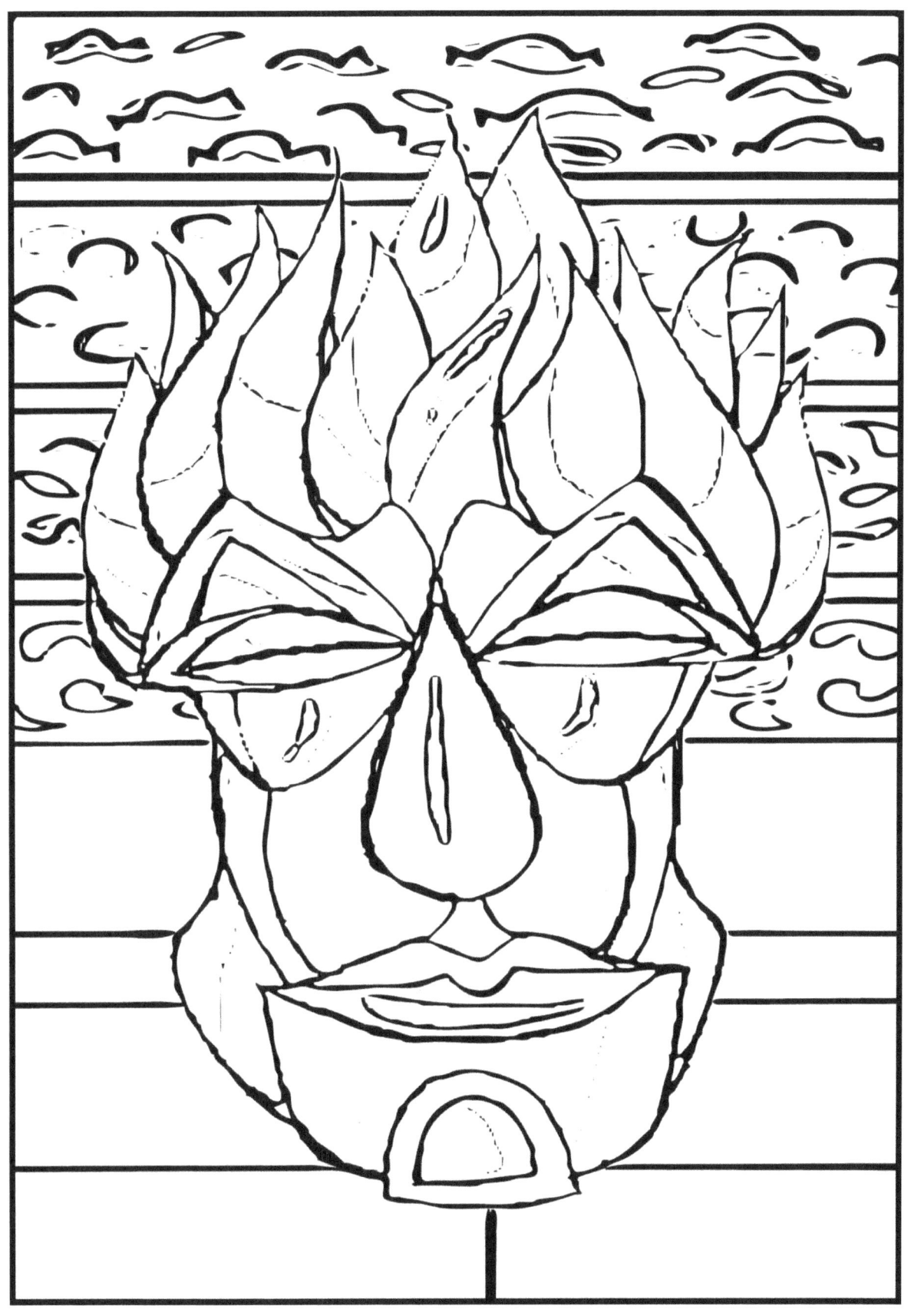

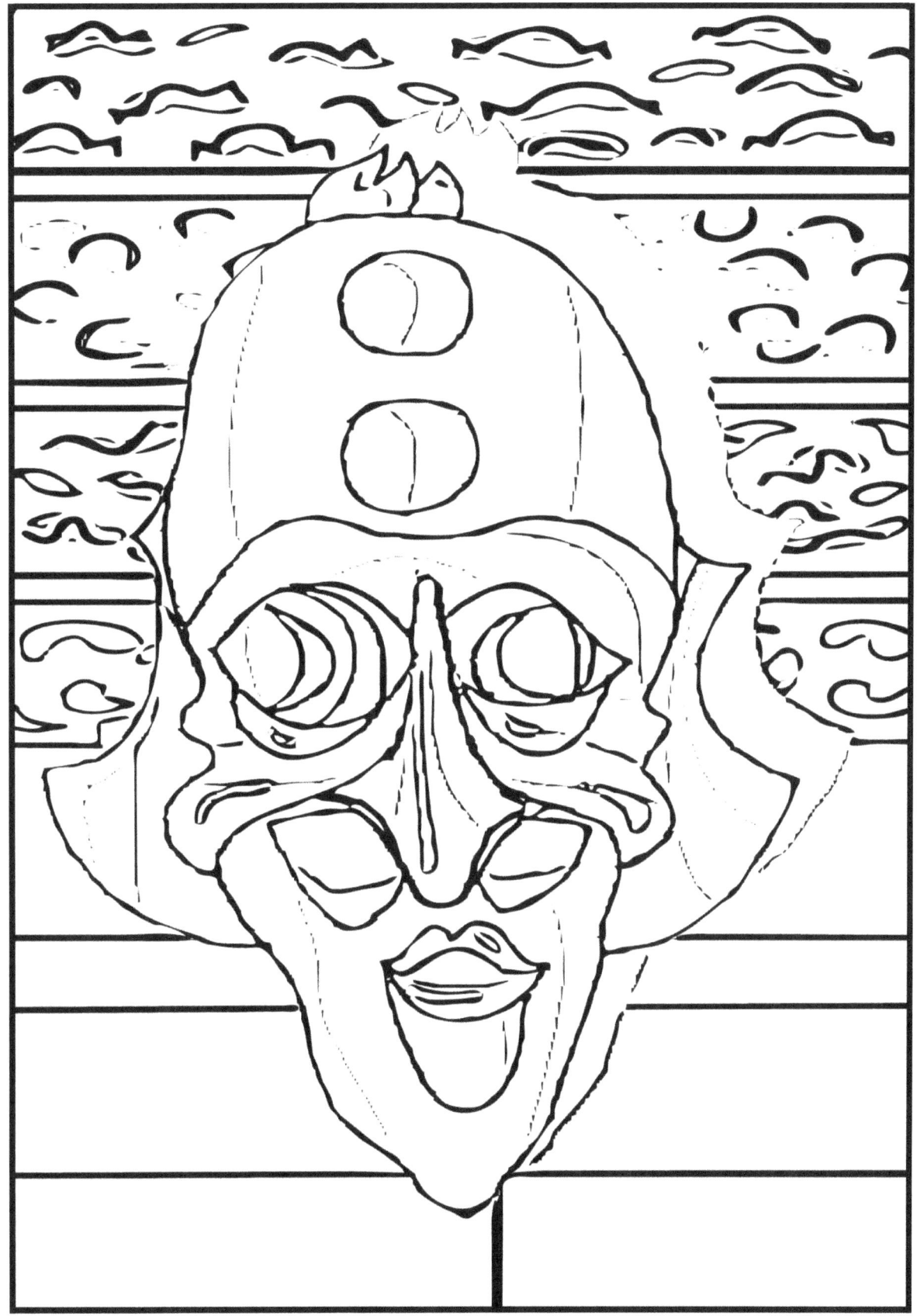

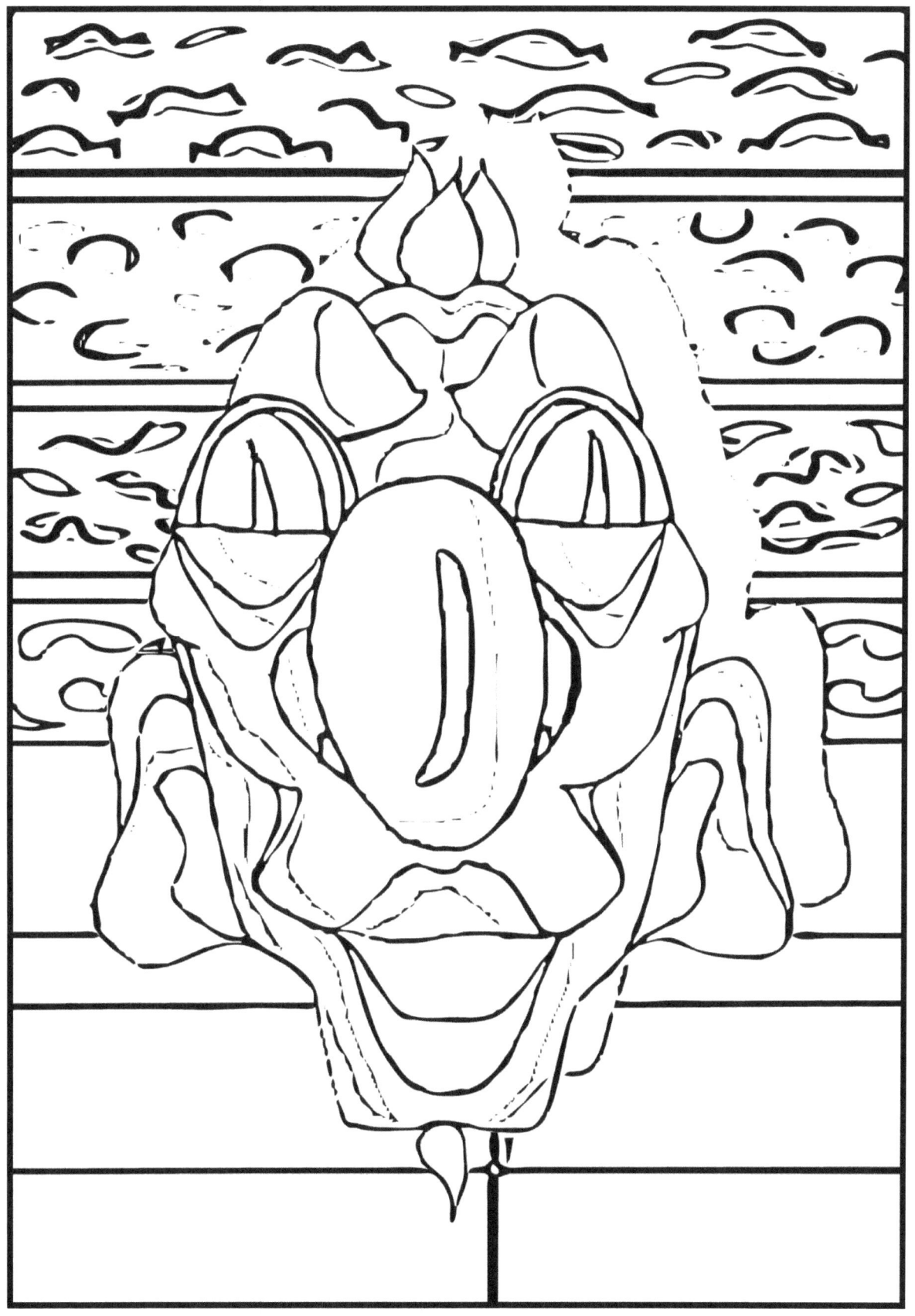

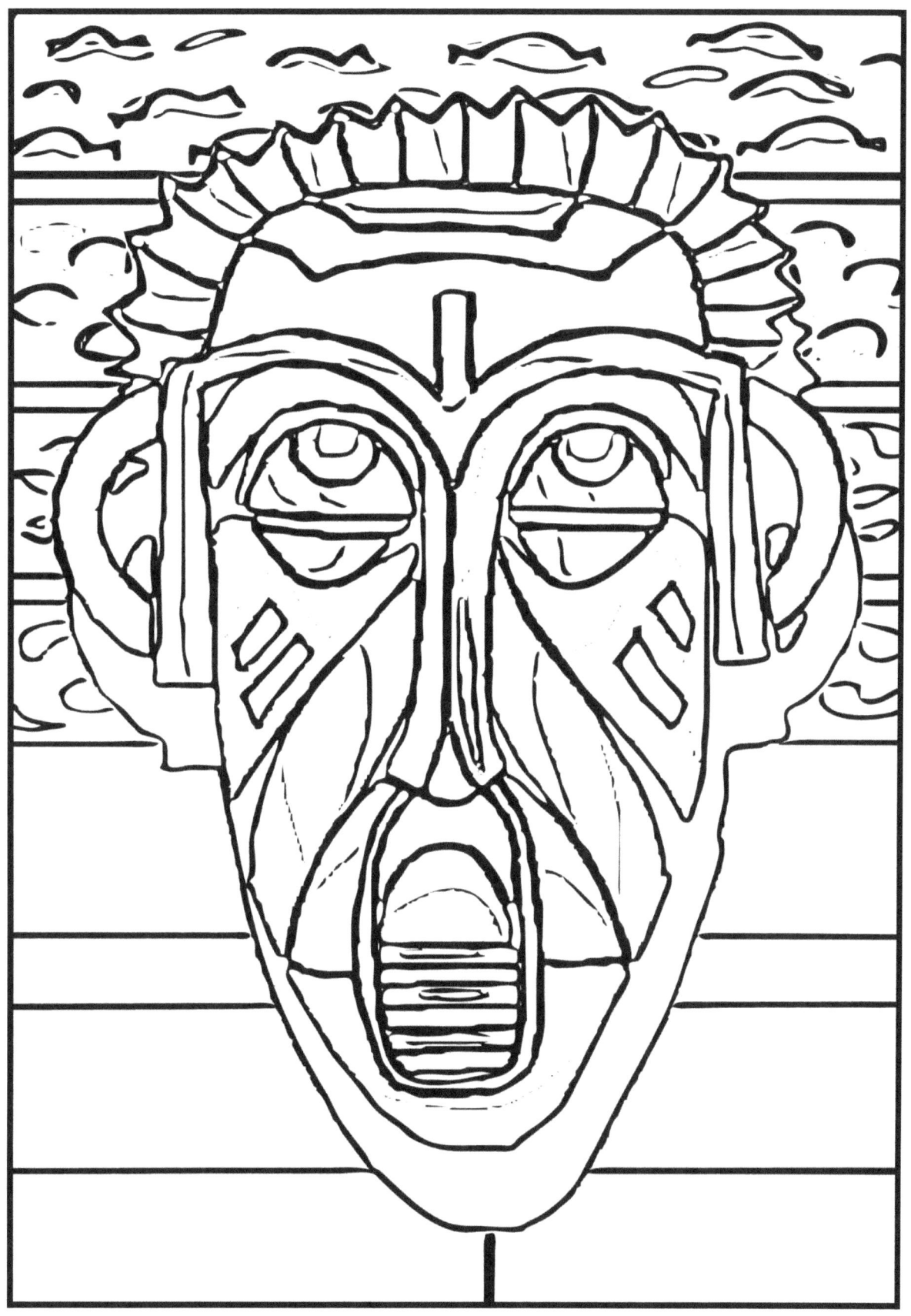

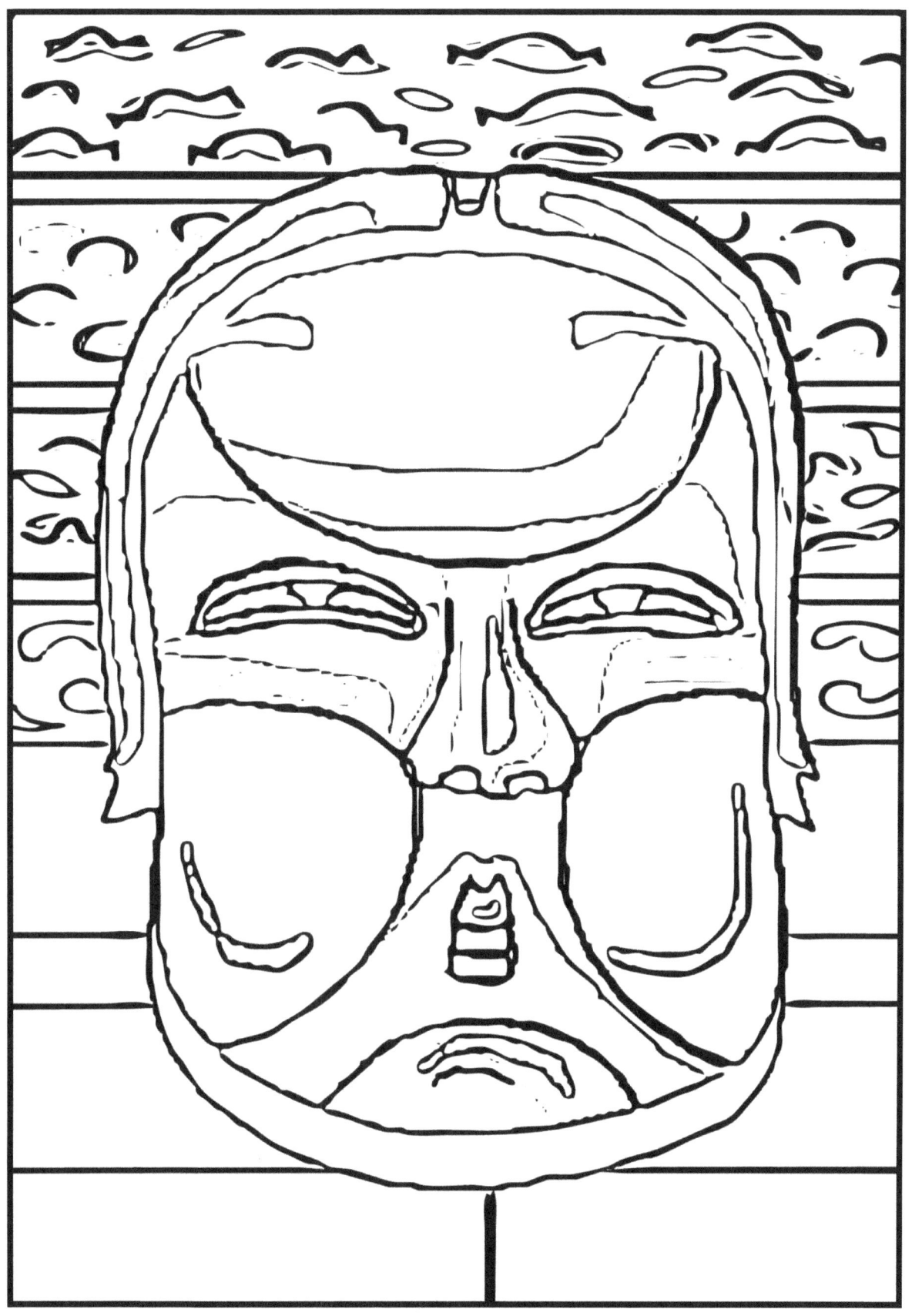

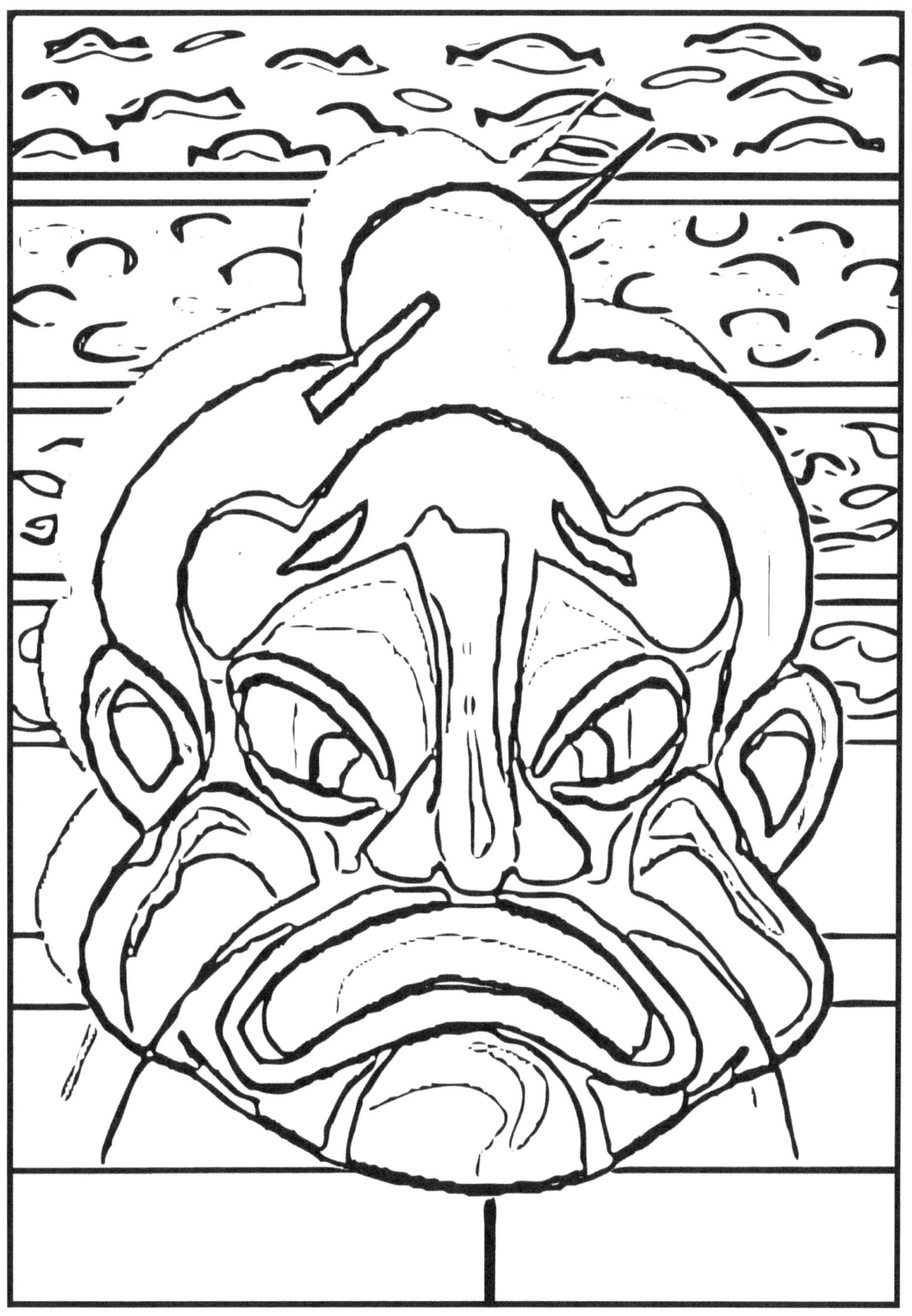

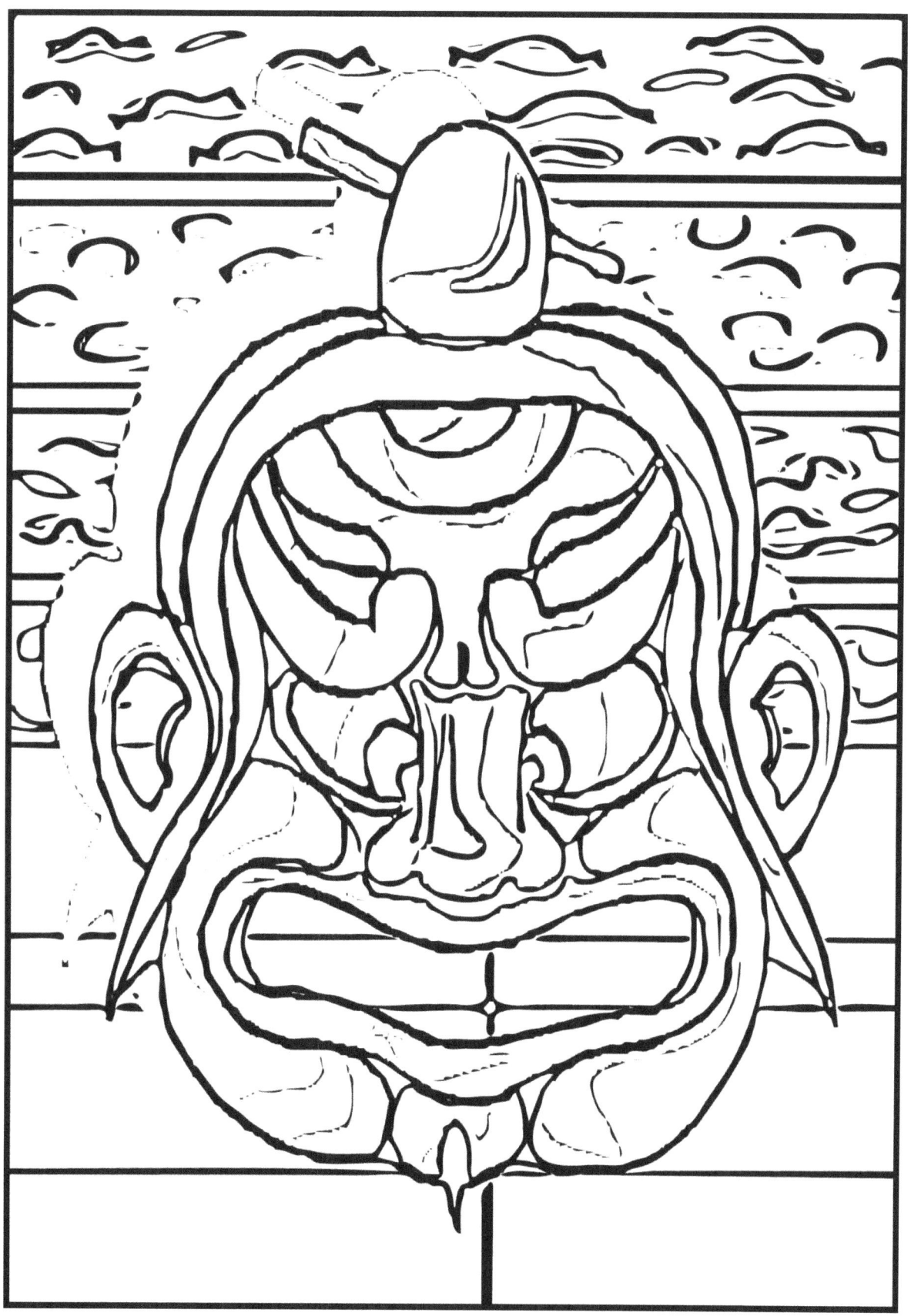

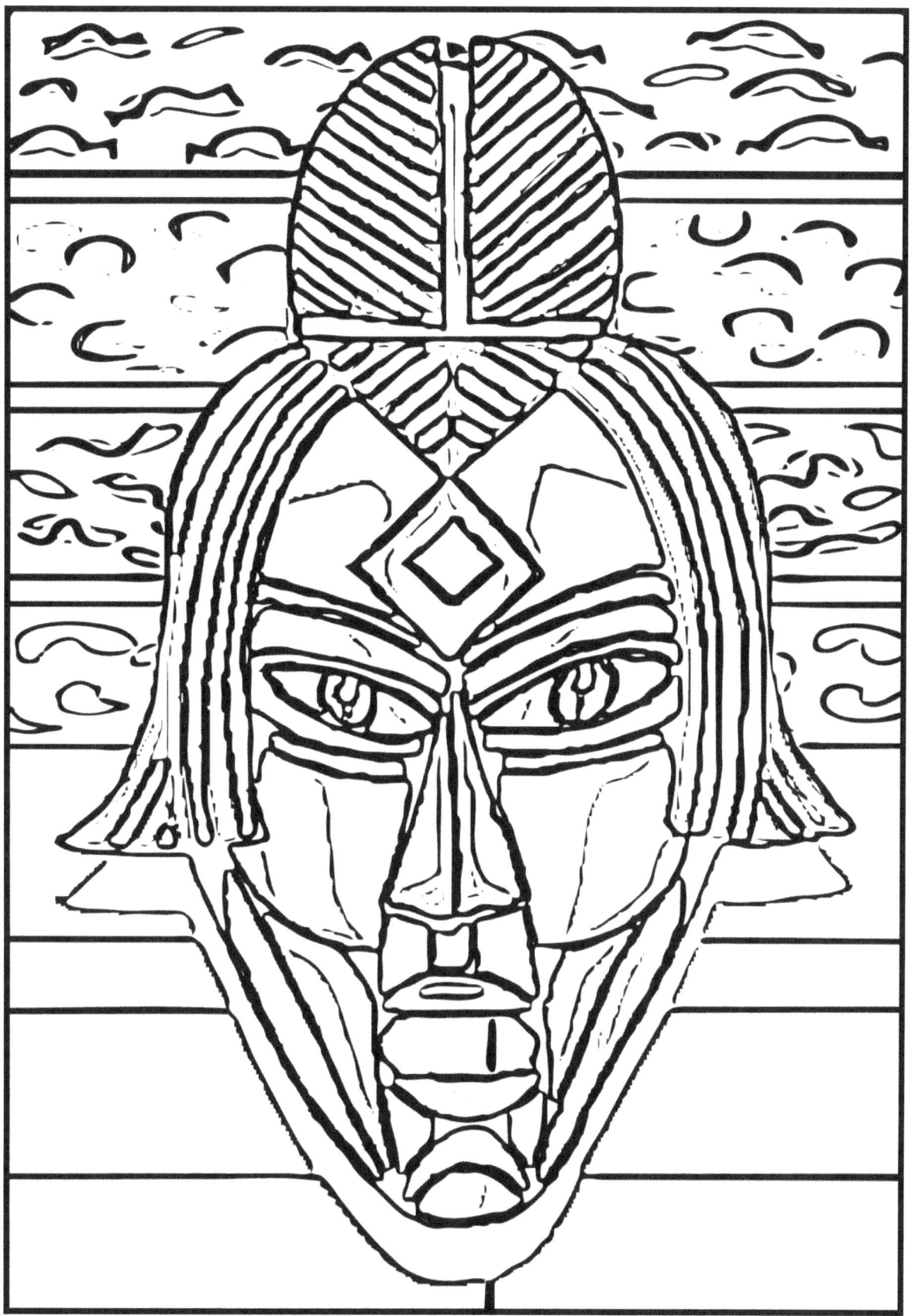

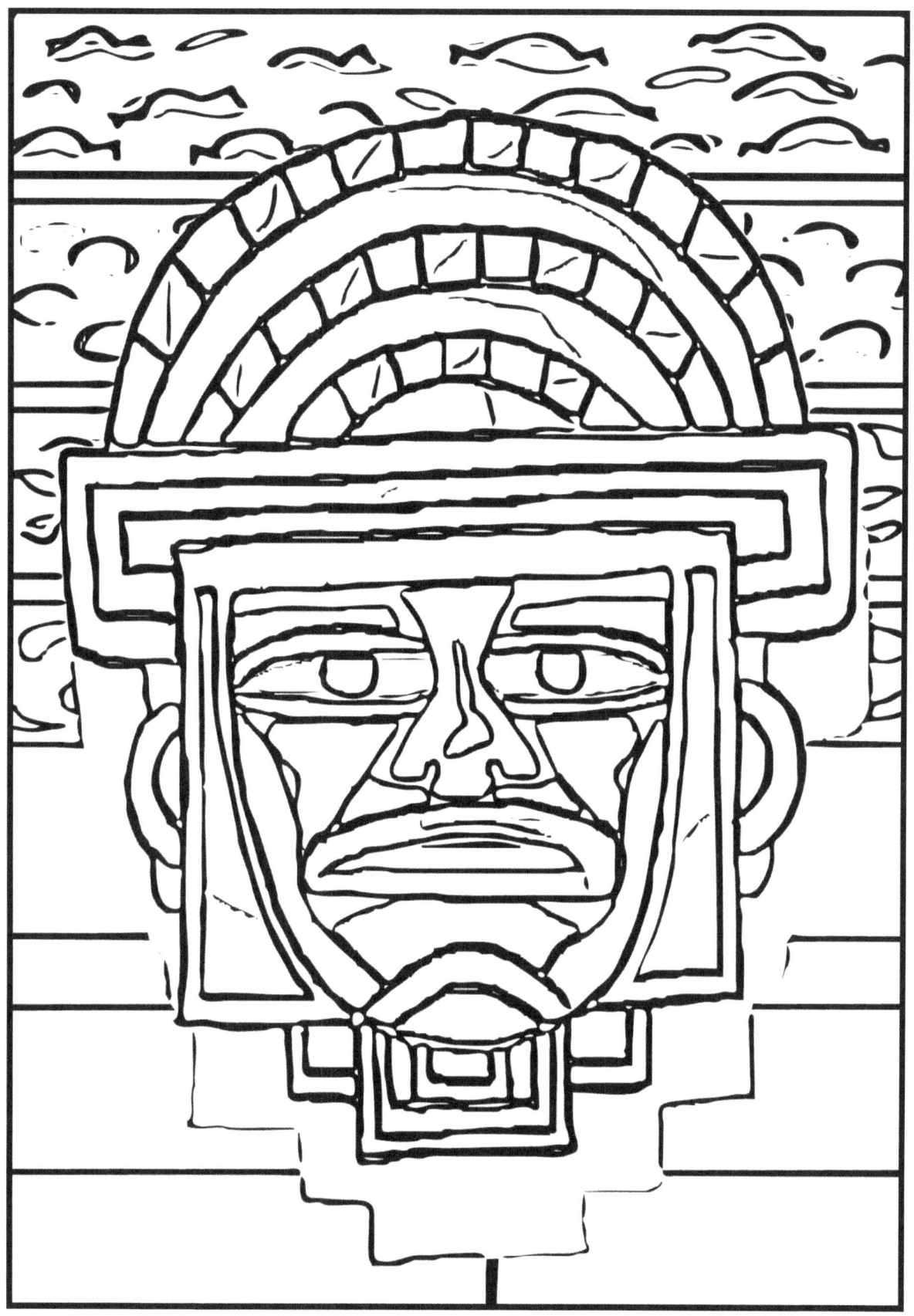

www.ingramcontent.com/pod-product-compliance
Lightning Source LLC
Chambersburg PA
CBHW081210180526
45170CB00006B/2285